ntial

Co Applications

Essential Computer Applications

Data-Bases, Spreadsheets, and Word-processing

Gerard Morgan and Séamus O'Neill

Gill and Macmillan

Published in Ireland by
Gill and Macmillan Ltd
Goldenbridge
Dublin 8
with associated companies in
Auckland, Budapest, Gaborone, Harare,
Hong Kong, Kampala, Kuala Lumpur, Lagos, London,
Madras, Manzini, Melbourne, Mexico City, Nairobi,
New York, Singapore, Sydney, Tokyo, Windhoek
© Gerard Morgan and Séamus O'Neill 1991
Reprinted twice 1992
Designed by
The Unlimited Design Company, Dublin
Print origination by Seton Music Graphics, Bantry, Co. Cork
Printed in Hong Kong

British Library Cataloguing in Publication Data
Morgan, Gerard
    Essential computer applications: data-bases,
    spreadsheets, and word-processing.
    I. Title II. O'Neill, Séamus
    005.3

ISBN 0–7171–1884–3

Contents

Acknowledgments

We would like to acknowledge all the people who made this book possible, in particular: Mr Philip Galvin, Principal, Crumlin College of Business and Technical Studies, for use of the college computer facilities; the staff and students of Crumlin College for their co-operation, especially classes CB1 and CDN for their tireless testing of assignments; Mr A. Clifford, Mr D. Cooney, Mr D. Cox and Mr J.T. Smyth for their advice and encouragement; Mr Hubert Mahony and all the staff of Gill and Macmillan.

From G. Morgan, special thanks to my wife, Mary, for her continuous help and encouragement.

Students on Information Technology courses such as the following will find this book useful:

City and Guilds 7261: Wordprocessing (400), Database (401), Spreadsheet (402), Microcomputers and Business Applications (405);

RSA CLAIT I and II;

BTEC First, BTEC National;

AAT and IOB Preliminary Level;

PEI Intermediate;

LCCI examinations.

Dedicated to our parents

Section A

Chapter 1

An essential overview

Before deciding to explore the three application areas outlined in this book, we must have some basic background knowledge of computing. To use a comparison: before beginning to drive a car on the road we need to have some idea of the working of gears and other equipment in the car. We also need to know the rules of the road. Similarly, before using computers we should know about the equipment and procedures we are likely to use.

This chapter will cover the following areas:

A. Hardware: computer equipment
1. Types of computer systems
2. Parts of a typical microcomputer system
3. The four-stage model of a computer
4. Input hardware
5. Processing hardware
6. Output hardware
7. Auxiliary storage
8. Hardware summary

B. Software: computer programs
1. The operating system
2. Application programs
3. Types of application programs

A. Hardware: computer equipment

A **computer** is a programmable electronic device that can store and process information and display the results.

The term 'hardware' is often used to refer to any physical part of a computer system, such as the keyboard, the monitor, the printer, or the disk drive.

1. Types of computer systems

Computer systems are usually divided into three main types according to their size.

Mainframe computers

Mainframe computers (or 'mainframes') are large, powerful computers that many people can use at the same time. They are also the most expensive systems. They are used for very large processing tasks, and perform many important business and Government applications.

Minicomputers

These are smaller and more compact systems, and fewer operators can use them compared with a mainframe computer. They are usually found in medium-sized businesses or in divisions within a large organisation, for example in Government departments.

Microcomputers

Microcomputers—also called 'personal computers'—are small, self-contained computers that fit on a desk-top and are usually only used by one person. They are the least expensive type, and are widely used in businesses for a variety of tasks, such as word-processing, small data-base management, and spreadsheets. They are also used as home computers, for family budgeting and similar jobs, as well as for games.

For the purposes of this book we will be concentrating on microcomputers. However, much of the information here is also applicable to other computer systems. Also, as computers become more powerful and at the same time smaller, this division by size is becoming less useful. In particular, the distinction between mainframe computers and minicomputers is sometimes hard to draw; while at the same time a number of microcomputers joined together or 'networked' can perform many of the functions associated with minicomputers.

2. Parts of a typical microcomputer system

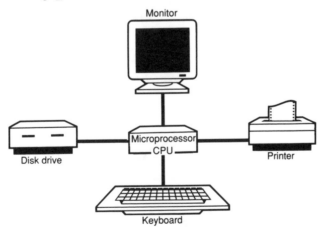

The **keyboard** is used to get the information into the computer. The **CPU** is used to process this information: for example to do calculations. The **monitor** is used to display the result; and the **printer** produces a copy of this display. The **disk drives** make it possible for the information (and programs) to be stored on disks for further use.

3. The four-stage model of a computer

In general, then, we can say that a computer has four main components:

- the hardware used to enter data, called **input devices**
- the hardware that produces results from entered data, called the **processor**
- the hardware that displays the results, called **output devices**
- the hardware used to store this information for later retrieval, called **auxiliary storage** or backing storage

All the pieces of hardware outside the processor are called **peripherals.**

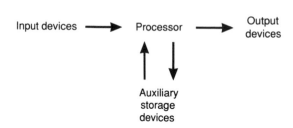

4. Input hardware

Keyboard

This is the most common means of entering data. It consists of an array of **keys** or switches, each one producing a particular character on the display when it is pressed. The character keys have a standard layout on all computer keyboards, called the 'QWERTY' layout after the first six letters on the top row; additional keys can include **cursor keys, function keys**, and **editing keys.** The 'enter' key is used to implement a command or, in word-processing, to mark the end of a paragraph. The 'escape' key is often used to cancel an operation.

Mouse

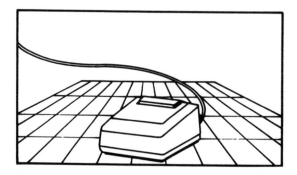

This is a small **pointing device** connected by a wire to the computer (it vaguely resembles a real mouse!). It is moved about by hand on a flat surface, and the cursor on the screen follows its movements. Buttons on the top of the mouse can also be used to select options. *Where used*: various 'user-friendly' (easy-to-use) programs, especially graphics.

Scanner

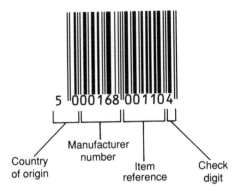

Most consumer products now have **bar codes** on them. A scanner can read these codes by scanning the pattern of lines; this allows the product code to be entered without keyboarding. *Where used:* supermarkets; libraries.

Light-pen

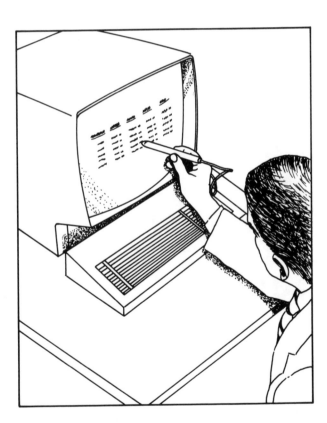

This is another pointing device, resembling a pen with a small light on the end. It is used to point to parts of a display to select options. *Where used:* some 'user-friendly' applications, especially graphics.

Magnetic card reader

This a machine that reads data from the magnetic strip on a plastic card. *Where used:* cash dispensing machines; employee access to buildings.

Kimball tags

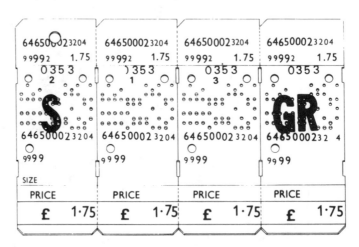

These are small price-tags that contain encoded data in the form of small punched holes. The tags are retained when an item is purchased, and can be read using a Kimball tag reader. Light is used to read the holes on the tag; the different light patterns determine the product code entered into the computer. *Where used:* shops, particularly clothes shops.

Voice data entry (VDE)

Using a microphone connected to the computer, different commands or letters (usually up to two hundred) can be called out and then interpreted by special programs. *Where used:* laboratories; computers for the physically handicapped.

Optical character recognition (OCR)

```
0 1 2 3 4 5 6 7 8 9
A B C D E F G H I J
K L M N O P Q R S T
U V W X Y Z

0123456789
ABCDEFGHIJ
KLMNOPQRST
UVWXYZ
abcdefghij
klmnopqrst
uvwxyz
```

This is an input method where a scanner is used to read the text of a document directly into the computer. Special typefaces that the machine recognises can be used, although modern systems can now read ordinary typefaces. *Where used:* processing of customer bills that have been received with payment; reading of authors' typescripts directly into typesetting systems.

Magnetic-ink character recognition (MICR)

```
1 2 3 4 5 6 7 8
9 0 ⑈ ⑆ ⑇ ⑉
1234567890 ⑈⑆⑇⑉
```

Numerals of a special design can be printed with an ink that contains tiny pieces of magnetisable material, and these can then be read into the computer by a special scanner. The numbers along the bottom of a cheque are used by the computer to update a customer's bank account. They include code numbers representing the bank and branch, the customer account number, and the number of the cheque (printed on each page of the chequebook before it is issued to the customer), and the amount (printed on the cheque after it has been presented to the bank). *Where used:* chequebooks and other bank documents.

Optical mark recognition (OMR)

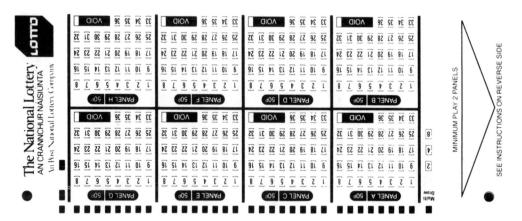

With this system a reader connected to the computer can detect the presence or absence of a mark, with the position of the mark determining the value entered. *Where used:* National Lottery; electricity meter reading; multi-choice examination questions.

Touch-sensitive screen

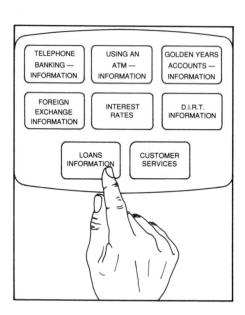

The screen displays choices and instructions, and the user simply touches the symbol representing the desired choice. *Where used:* information screens in banks and shopping centres.

There are many other methods of entering data into a computer for processing. The choice of the most suitable input device depends on the nature of the data to be entered and the environment where the data is generated.

5. Processing hardware

The central processing unit (CPU)

This is where all calculations and manipulations of the data are carried out: it could be considered the 'brain' of the computer. The CPU is contained on a tiny **integrated circuit** or 'microchip' that carries a large number of minute electronic circuits.

There are three main areas in the CPU: the control unit; the arithmetic and logic unit (ALU); and the main storage or 'memory'.

The **control unit** takes instructions in a given sequence (rather like a set of traffic lights at a crossroads) and controls the movement of data inside the computer.

The **arithmetic and logic unit** (ALU) performs mathematical functions and logical decisions, such as deciding whether one number is greater than another.

The **main storage** or 'memory' allows data to be stored for processing purposes, and holds the results. It also stores programs. It is something like our own memory. If you are asked to add three numbers without using pen and paper you would first have to put the numbers into your head, or memory, and then add them. So too with computers. In order to perform any calculations or processes the computer must first have in its memory the data that is required.

A microchip containing the control unit and the ALU is called a **microprocessor**.

Computer memory

There are two types of main storage: read-only memory (ROM) and random-access memory (RAM).

The **read-only memory** (ROM) contains information the computer permanently needs to have, for example the basic instructions essential for the operation of the computer. This information is entered at the time of manufacture and cannot be changed by the user. When the computer is turned off, this information is not lost; this form of storage is therefore referred to as 'non-volatile memory'. The information normally only takes up a small amount of the total memory of the computer.

The **random-access memory** (RAM) contains information being worked on at the present time. In our example above, the three numbers to be added would be contained in RAM while the calculation is being performed. Once the calculation has been completed new data can be entered into RAM. It is like a note-pad: the user can read the information from this memory and (unlike ROM) can change its contents. When the computer is switched off, however, this memory is completely cleared; this form of storage is known therefore as 'volatile memory'. Before you turn off your computer, always make sure to save your data if you want it for another day!

The representation of data

How is the data inside the computer represented? Computers can only understand the numerals 1 and 0, symbolising the presence (1) or absence (0) of an electrical pulse inside the computer. How, then, can they deal with other numbers, letters, and even words?

First of all each **character** (numeral, letter, or symbol) on the keyboard has its own code number. For example, the capital letter A is character number 65. (The character numbers are allocated by an international agreement, which was based on an earlier one called the American Standard Code for Information Interchange (ASCII), and they are often still called the ASCII code—pronounced 'askey'.) The character numbers do not have to be known by the user: the computer automatically reads them when each key is pressed.

The computer converts each character code into this 1 and 0 form, known as a **binary number**. For the letter A (character 65) this is 01000001. All the data inside the computer is made up of thousands of these pulses or no-pulses of electricity moving in and out of the memory very rapidly.

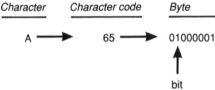

Each character is thus represented by a binary number, made up of a series of 1s and 0s. Each single 1 or 0 is called a **bit**, which is the smallest possible element in a computer memory. A group of bits of the size that a particular computer handles—usually eight—is called a **byte**.

Memory capacity

Computer capacity is expressed in terms of the maximum number of bytes or characters the computer can hold in RAM at any time for processing. This capacity is measured in a unit of 1,024 bytes, called a **kilobyte** (kb)—sometimes also referred to simply as 'k'—or a unit of 1,024 kilobytes, called a **megabyte** (Mb)—approximately 1 million bytes. Thus a computer that has a RAM of 32 kb can keep in its memory at any time a maximum of approximately 33,000 characters. Personal computers typically have RAM capacities ranging from 64 kb to 1 Mb.

Having more RAM available in a computer means that it can handle more data and can also accommodate larger applications programs, thus making it more useful for processing purposes. When buying a computer you should be sure that it has adequate memory capacity for your requirements.

Communication ports

At the back of all CPUs there are a number of connecting points called **ports**. These allow the computer to be connected to the keyboard and printer and to other peripheral devices. There are two types of port: serial and parallel.

A **serial port** is a connection point that sends information to or from the CPU one bit after another.

A **parallel port** is a connection point that sends information a byte at a time, i.e. in groups of eight bits.

A hardware device is said to be **on-line** when it is connected to the CPU of the computer and under its control. A device is **off-line** if it is not under the control of the CPU.

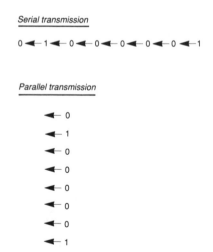

6. Output hardware

When information has been entered and processed by the computer, we obviously need to see the result. Output devices allow this data to be seen.

Monitor

The monitor, also called a visual display unit (VDU), is the most common means of displaying computer information. There are many sizes and types of monitor.

A **monochrome** screen displays only one colour, often green or amber on black, or black on white, whereas a colour screen can usually display up to sixteen different colours.

A **low-resolution screen,** mainly used to display text, has a relatively small number of 'pixels' (the dots that make up an image). A **high-resolution screen**, often used to display graphics, usually has more than 30,000 pixels. Examples of high-resolution displays are those of the VGA (video graphics adapter) or EGA (enhanced graphics adapter) types.

Instead of the traditional cathode-ray tube (CRT), some screens use a **liquid crystal display** (LCD), like that on digital watches and calculators. These screens are flat and more compact, and are often used for portable ('lap-top') computers.

The problem with LCD screens is that they cannot be seen if looked at from an angle. With **gas plasma** screens the display has a glow, allowing it to be seen from any angle, while also being compact.

Printers

The problem with a display is that it is only temporary: when the computer is switched off, the display is lost! Printers allow the information to be put onto paper, creating a permanent and portable display. The output from a printer on paper is called a **print-out** or sometimes 'hard copy'.

There are several types of computer printer. They are sometimes classified as **impact printers** (those that print characters by striking the paper through an inked ribbon: e.g. dot-matrix and daisy-wheel printers) and **non-impact printers** (those where the print head does not make contact with the paper: e.g. laser and ink-jet printers).

Computers — near letter quality

Computers — dot-matrix

The most popular printers are **dot-matrix** printers. These use a series of print combs that strike the ribbon to produce a character made up of a pattern of dots. These printers are cheap, but are quite slow, and do not usually produce high quality. The more dots making up the character the better the image; better dot-matrix printers can produce characters made up of twenty-four or more dots, and this output is described as **near-letter-quality** (NLQ).

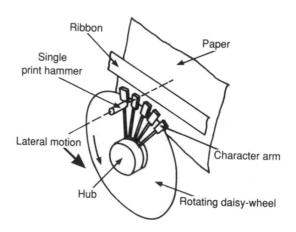

Daisy-wheel

The characters on **daisy-wheel printers** are moulded on the end of spokes that are arranged in a circle, like the petals of a flower—hence the name! When printing, the wheel rotates until the required character is beneath the hammer in the print head. The hammer strikes the character, which in turn strikes the paper through the ribbon. The output from these printers is said to be 'letter-quality': this means that the characters are fully formed, continuous lines produced to the standard of a traditional typewriter.

The mode of operation of **laser printers** is similar to that of photocopiers. They produce very high-quality printing and are extremely fast; however, they are expensive to buy and to run.

In **ink-jet printers** a finely controlled jet of ink is sprayed at the paper. The characters are made using dots similar to the characters produced by dot-matrix printers, but to a higher quality.

The output of low-speed printers is measured by the number of characters they can print per second. The output of high-speed printers is usually measured in pages per minute.

Printers compared			
Type	Printing speed	Quality	Applications
Dot-matrix	30–600 char/s	Poor to NLQ	Draft printing and low-speed NLQ
Daisy-wheel	15–150 char/s	Letter quality	Low-volume high-quality applications
Laser	5–10 page/min (4,000 char/s)	Letter quality	High-volume high-quality applications
Ink-jet	25–250 char/s	Letter quality or NLQ	Low-volume quiet output

Printer paper

Most printers can use two types of paper: fan-fold paper, and sheets.

Fan-fold paper consists of one long sheet perforated at intervals and folded alternately backwards and forwards on the perforations. It is fed into the printer by means of the small holes on the side of the paper (this is called 'tractor feed'). After printing, the sections are pulled apart to form pages of standard (usually A4) size.

Using a 'form feeder', individual sheets of paper, usually A4 size, can be fed into the printer from a tray like that on a photocopier.

7. Auxiliary storage

Do we have to type in all the information the computer needs each time a task has to be performed? No! All computer systems can store information for later retrieval. Magnetic disks of various types and sizes are the most common storage medium.

Diskettes or 'floppy disks'

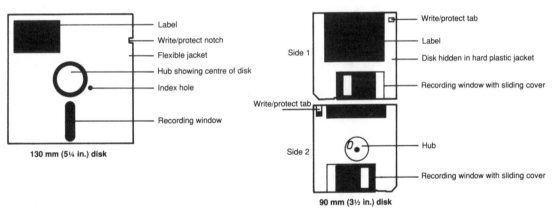

Diskettes are small disks made of flexible plastic that is coated with a magnetisable material. These disks are removed from the **disk drive** when not in use, and can be copied, filed, carried around, or even sent through the post.

The first microcomputer disks had a diameter of 130 mm (5.25 in.) and were enclosed in a strong but flexible plastic envelope (hence the term 'floppy disk'). The modern standard disk has a diameter of 90 mm (3.5 in.) and is completely enclosed in a rigid plastic cartridge—although disks of the earlier type continue to be used side-by-side with the newer ones.

The information on the disk is stored in the form of spots of magnetisable material, each spot representing one bit (magnetised = 1, unmagnetised = 0). This information is stored on **tracks** or concentric rings on the disk. There are usually forty tracks on a 130 mm disk and eighty tracks on a 90 mm disk.

Most disks are **double-sided** (2S), i.e. they have a usable surface on both sides. The amount of information that can be packed onto a disk varies: for example, a 130 mm (5.25 in.) double-sided **double-density** (2S-2D) disk usually holds about 360 kb; a 90 mm (3.5 in.) 2S-2D disk usually holds about 720 kb. A **high-density** (HD) disk holds more again.

Fixed disks or 'hard disks'

Fixed disks (usually called 'hard disks', in contrast to 'floppy disks') are permanently installed inside the case of the computer. They are made of a hard metal alloy with a magnetisable coating on both sides. These disks can store very large quantities of information, some up to a hundred times more than a diskette. They can also access this information much faster.

Optical disks

Optical disks are physically similar to the compact disks (CDs) used by the recording industry. They can store up to a hundred times the amount of information on a fixed disk. The only problem with these disks is that the user can only read information from the disk: it is not possible to record your own information on them. Such disks are often referred to as 'write once, read many times' (WORM) disks.

Comparison of some typical disk densities		
Type	Size	Capacity
Diskettes	130 mm 2S-2D	360 kb
	90 mm 2S-2D	720 kb
	90 mm 2S-HD	1.4 Mb
Fixed disks	130 mm	10–70 Mb
Optical disks	300 mm	800 Mb

Formatting a disk

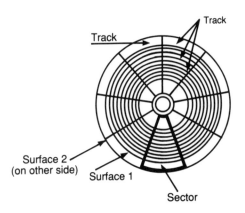

A disk is formatted only once—before using it for the first time—and simply divides the disk into **sectors** or slices. The procedure is similar to dividing a city into postal districts: the sectors allow data to be stored on specific areas on the disk for easy retrieval.

For example, when a file or document is stored on the disk it will have to be given a file name. Along with this name the computer will keep a record of where it recorded that file on the disk. For example, the **file name** might be CAR. When this file is saved the file name will be recorded on the outer track ('file allocation table') of the disk as CAR 712. This track is used to tell the computer where it has stored the file on the disk: 7 means the seventh sector and 12 means the twelfth track. When the computer needs to retrieve this data it will immediately position the **read-write head** (like the stylus of a record player) at the twelfth track in the seventh sector.

This method of positioning the read-write head exactly on the spot where the data is stored is called **direct access**. This allows information to be retrieved from disks very rapidly.

Care of disks

Magnetic disks must be treated with great care. The following is a list of ideal conditions for storage and handling.

- The atmosphere should not be damp
- Always store disks in a box in the upright position
- Keep 130 mm (5.25 in.) 'floppy' disks in their protective envelopes when not in use
- Do not leave disks in direct sunlight or near direct heat sources
- Do not expose disks to magnetic fields, by leaving them near magnets or electric motors
- Do not place heavy objects on disks
- Keep solvents away from disks
- The storage temperature should be between 10 and 45 °C—the ideal is room temperature, about 30 °C.

From this it can be seen how easily disks could be damaged. For this reason, and because of possible loss of data from wear and tear on disks or power failure or hardware problems, you should keep contingency or 'back-up' copies of all data and program files. Back-up disks (which are exact copies of original disks) should be regularly updated, and used only in an emergency.

Other storage media

Magnetic tape, similar to that used in tape recorders, can also be used to store computer information. For some small home computers, audio tape cassettes can be used in a standard tape recorder-player. For business use, reel-to-reel tapes are used.

The main disadvantage of tapes is that only **serial access** is available, compared with the direct access possible with disks. This means that the tape must be wound forward until it reaches the spot where the information is stored, which can take several minutes in certain circumstances.

Magnetic tape is not used very often with business microcomputers, except occasionally for contingency or 'back-up' purposes.

8. Hardware summary

Input	Process	Output
Keyboard Document reader —OCR —OMR —MICR Mouse Light-pen Kimball tag reader Magnetic card reader VDE Touch-sensitive screen	**CPU** Control unit ALU Main storage **Auxiliary storage** Disk-drives —Diskette 　　　　　—Fixed disk 　　　　　—Optical disk Tape drive —Cassette tape 　　　　　—Reel-to-reel	Monitor Printer —Laser —Dot-matrix —Daisy-wheel —Ink-jet

B. Software: computer programs

So far we have discussed the machinery or equipment that makes up a computer system: the 'hardware'. The problem is that if we had all this equipment available to us the computer would still be useless. So what is missing? The programs or 'software'.

The software is the system of instructions that enables the computer to perform its function. A car is useless without instructions to go fast or slow, stop or start. So too a computer is useless without the instructions for performing a particular task. For example, if we want to extract a trial balance from a computer we must first have the accounting program (instructions) in the computer.

There are two types of software that need to be in place before we can use the computer: the operating system, and application programs.

1. The operating system

This is the system of instructions that looks after the internal running of the computer: procedures for displaying information on the screen, reading from disks, listing the contents of the disk, and so on. A common operating system used with IBM microcomputers and other computers based on this design is the Microsoft Disk Operating System (MSDOS—pronounced 'em-ess-doss'). Other types of microcomputer, such as the Apple Macintosh, have their own operating systems.

These instructions must be in the computer's memory before any other software can function. Programs work by communicating requests to the operating system, which acts as a kind of secretary to the user and the user's programs.

2. Application programs

Programs are systems of instructions that are written to make the computer perform specific tasks, such as

- word-processing
- spreadsheets
- graphics
- data-base management
- financial accounting
- sales order processing

Programs that perform specific functions such as these are often called **applications** (to distinguish them from programs that make the computer itself work more effectively, called **utilities**). Application programs are written in computer programming languages by large specialist companies, such as Microsoft, Lotus, Claris, and Ashton-Tate, and these programs can then be bought 'off the shelf' from computer suppliers. Alternatively, computer programs can be specially written (or customised) for a particular company's needs: this kind of program can be very expensive.

3. Types of application programs

Programs are often described as either menu-driven or command-driven (though sometimes they may be a mixture of the two). In **command-driven** programs the user has to type in a command, consisting of a special series of keystrokes, in order to run the program or to call up its different features; other commands might be invoked by pressing the function keys. Examples include the control commands of Wordstar and the function keys of Wordperfect.

With **menu-driven** programs, choices are made from a list or 'menu' of the operations possible at each stage, often by means of a mouse. This is becoming the most popular type of program, as it is so easy to use. Examples of menu-driven software are Pegasus Accounts, Dbase 3 Plus, and Microsoft Windows, and all programs on Apple Macintosh computers.

Easy-to-use programs

Greater emphasis is placed nowadays on programs that are easy to learn and to use, or 'user-friendly'. Some or all of the following features may be found with such programs:

Sound: Sound may be used to signal to the user that a mistake has been made. Sound may also indicate that a task is complete or that the computer is awaiting more data.

Colour or contrast: Colour can highlight displays and improve the presentation of information. With a monochrome monitor, changes in contrast can be used instead to highlight various options.

Help facility: The user can give a special command to request help if needed. With some programs, if an error occurs the computer will automatically give the required explanation and offer ways to remedy the mistake. This is called 'on-line help'.

Icons: These are small symbols displayed on the screen to represent commands or options, and are usually selected by using a mouse. This means that complex commands do not have to be remembered.

Menus: The use of menus means that the user is guided through the application.

Program prompts: At no stage during the operation of a program should the user be left not knowing what to do next or in what form the information should be entered. Program prompts are messages telling the user the next action to take or offering a choice, such as 'Press any key to continue' or 'Do you want to exit the system (Y/N)?'

On the other hand sound, graphics or colour may not enhance the ease of use of a particular program. Frequent beeps may be a source of irritation to the user, and may distract others working in the same room. The graphics and colour may only serve to cause eye discomfort.

Summary

In order to use a computer you must have both the 'hardware' or computer equipment and the 'software' or computer instructions to perform a particular task or set of tasks.

Questions

Multi-choice questions

1. Which of the following is the smallest computer system?

   (a) megacomputer
   (b) minicomputer
   (c) mainframe
   (d) microcomputer

2. A monitor is—

   (a) an output device
   (b) an input device
   (c) a peripheral device
   (d) an item of hardware
   (e) all of the above?

3. The CPU consists of—

    (a) control unit, ALU, and main storage
    (b) ROM, RAM, and ALU
    (c) main storage
    (d) chips?

4. ROM is—

    (a) non-volatile
    (b) storage
    (c) permanently required
    (d) all of the above?

5. Typically, how many bits are there in one byte?

    (a) 4
    (b) 2
    (c) 65
    (d) 8

6. Which of the following disks holds most information?

    (a) 130 mm (5.25 in.) disk
    (b) 90 mm (3.5 in.) disk
    (c) fixed (hard) disk
    (d) optical disk?

7. Formatting a disk is usually done—

    (a) once before using a new disk
    (b) every time something is saved on the disk
    (c) every time the disk is full
    (d) to make a back-up copy of a file?

8. The instructions that enable a computer to function are called—

    (a) hardware
    (b) applications
    (c) software
    (d) instructions?

9. Which one of the following printers cannot produce letter-quality printing?

    (a) laser printer
    (b) ink-jet printer
    (c) dot-matrix printer
    (d) daisy-wheel printer

10. Which pair are the most commonly used input and output devices?

    (a) mouse, printer
    (b) keyboard, printer
    (c) VDE, monitor
    (d) keyboard, monitor

Short-answer questions

1. Name the three types of computer system, and give an example of where each system is normally used.
2. What is an input device? Name six different input devices.
3. How is data inside the computer's memory represented?
4. What units is computer capacity measured in?
5. What is a port?
6. What type of paper can a printer use?
7. List conditions likely to damage disks.
8. What is the function of the operating system, and how does it differ from application software?
9. What do the terms 'on-line' and 'off-line' mean? Give examples of on-line and off-line devices.
10. Explain the functions of ROM and RAM, and how they differ.

Glossary of computer terms

ALU (arithmetic and logic unit): the part of the CPU that performs mathematical functions and logical decisions, such as deciding whether one number is greater than another.

application software: programs to perform specific tasks, such as word-processing or data-base management, as distinct from system software (operating system), which maintains and organises the computer system.

ASCII (American Standard Code for Information Interchange): a term sometimes used to describe the system of allocating code numbers to different characters.

auxiliary ('backing') storage device: hardware used to store information for later retrieval.

bar code: a distinctive pattern of lines printed on a product or label, usually containing a code for the product number and capable of being entered into the computer by means of a suitable scanner.

binary number: a number system using only the digits 1 and 0, and therefore capable of being represented inside a computer by means of the presence (1) or absence (0) of an electrical current or magnetic charge.

bit: one digit in a binary number, either 1 or 0: the minimum unit of information in a computer system.

byte: a collection of bits, usually eight, to represent a single character.

catalogue: a listing of details of the files stored on a disk.

character: any of the signs used in creating text, whether letters, numerals, or symbols.

computer: a machine that processes data and supplies results.

contingency ('back-up') copy: a duplicate of data or program files kept in case of loss of this information; should be up-dated regularly and only used in an emergency.

control unit: the part of the CPU that takes instructions in a given sequence and controls the movement of data inside the computer.

corruption: the accidental alteration of data stored on any storage medium.

CPU (central processing unit): the part of the computer that decodes instructions and controls the hardware used to execute them; it consists of the control unit, arithmetic unit, and main storage (memory).

cursor: a movable mark on the screen that shows where the next character will be displayed.

cursor keys: a group of keys that move the cursor left, right, up or down the display.

default: an automatic option or value in a program that is used unless an alternative is specified (this term should not be confused with a fault of any kind).

direct access: a type of access used when reading information from a disk; the read-write head goes directly to the place on the disk where the data is stored.

directory: another term for 'catalogue'.

disk drive: an auxiliary storage device that enables data and programs to be stored and retrieved.

diskette/'floppy disk': a flexible plastic disk coated with a magnetisable material and enclosed in a plastic envelope or case.

dot-matrix printer: a printer that produces characters made up of patterns of dots.

editing keys: a group of keys that perform specialised functions such as page up, page down, go to end of file, etc.

fixed (hard) disk: a rigid, non-removable disk coated in a magnetisable material.

formatting: the procedure used to prepare a blank disk before use for a particular computer; it divides the disk into sectors so that information can be stored and retrieved.

function keys: a group of keys that can be programmed to execute commands or to choose options.

hardware: the physical components of a computer system.

input device: any hardware device that enables data to be transmitted from the source into the computer.

keyboard: an input device with a systematic arrangement of keys, used for entering instructions and data.

kilobyte (kb): a unit of 1,024 bytes (sometimes rounded to 1,000).

Kimball tag reader: an input device that reads small cards with encoded data that are used to record sales.

laser printer: a high-quality printer that uses a method of reproduction similar to a photocopier and prints whole pages at a time.

light-pen: an input device used in conjunction with a screen to choose commands or data.

mainframe computer: the largest type of computer, capable of being used by many people at the same time.

megabyte (Mb): a unit of 1,048,576 bytes (sometimes rounded to 1 million).

menu: a list of the options available at any stage in the execution of a program.

MICR (magnetic-ink character recognition): an input system that allows magnetic characters (usually found on cheques) to be read into a computer.

microcomputer: a self-contained desk-top computer built around a microprocessor and that can be used by only one person at a time; sometimes called a 'personal computer' (PC).

microprocessor: an integrated circuit or 'microchip' that contains the ALU and control unit of a computer.

minicomputer: a medium-sized computer system, usually used by one department or a medium-sized company.

monitor: an output device like a television set that shows the stages in the operation of a program and displays the results; sometimes called a 'visual display unit' (VDU).

mouse: an input device housed in a palm-sized case used for pointing to commands or icons on the screen; the movement of the mouse on the desk-top corresponds to the movement of the cursor on the display, and one or more buttons on the mouse can be used to select options or execute commands.

NLQ (near-letter-quality): a simulation of high-quality printing on a dot-matrix printer.

OCR (optical character recognition): an input system that reads printed or typewritten characters.

off-line: not under the direct control of the CPU.

OMR (optical mark recognition): an input device that can recognise the presence or absence of a mark.

on-line: under the control of the CPU.

operating system: all the software used to operate and maintain the computer system and utilities.

optical disk: an auxiliary storage device similar to a compact disk.

output device: any hardware device that enables computer data to be displayed, transmitted, or printed.

parallel port: a communications port that allows information to be received or transmitted in groups of bits.

port/communications port: an external socket allowing peripheral devices to be connected to a computer.

printer: an output device that produces printed text or graphics on paper.

RAM (random-access memory): an area of electronic storage inside the computer used to hold current data and programs; information is constantly read from and written to this memory area.

ROM (read-only memory): an area of electronic storage used to hold instructions essential to the running of the computer; it is not possible to write to this area.

scanner: an input device used to scan a pattern of lines such as that of a bar code.

serial access: a method of access used with magnetic tape, where files are stored one after another and information is retrieved by rapid winding or rewinding until the required files are found.

serial port: a communications port that allows bits of data to be received or transmitted one after the other.

software: another name for programs.

track: one of the concentric rings of data on a magnetic disk.

VDE (voice data entry): an input system that responds to the human voice.

VDU (visual display unit): another name for a monitor.

Section B

Data-bases

Chapter 2

Introduction to data-bases

What is the next available flight to New York? What is the current exchange rate for the Canadian dollar? Are there any rooms available at a certain hotel?

To answer these questions we may have to consult a travel agent, a bank clerk, and the hotel receptionist, respectively. It is unlikely, however, that they will know these answers immediately. They may have to consult their respective data-bases.

What is a data-base?

A data-base is an organised collection of related information. It usually consists of one or more files that may be related to one another.

What is a file?

A file is a collection of similar records.

An employment agency, Bestmatch Recruitment, holds a personnel file on people looking for suitable employment. For simplicity, we will assume that there are only six people on the agency's file at present:

NAME	ADDRESS	PHONE_NO	SEX	JOB	YEARS
MURPHY P	6 GREENORE PK	4449234	M	SECRETARY	2
HOPKIRK L	16 KILKENNY RD	8349042	F	SECRETARY	3
MAHER K	56 MAIN ST	8899593	M	CHEF	0
GREENE A	55 WICKLOW RD	5231772	F	ACCOUNTANT	10
BURNS J	57 HAZEL RD	7783924	M	CHEF	2
OWENS M	56 ASHE ST	4931448	F	PHARMACIST	4

The information on each of the people seeking suitable employment is arranged under these headings:

NAME: the person's name (surname and initial);

ADDRESS: the person's home address;

PHONE_NO: the person's home telephone number;

SEX: the person's sex;

JOB: the job sought;

YEARS: the number of years' experience the person has at this work.

(Note that there is an underline character rather than a space in 'PHONE_NO': this is because some data-base programs need the parts of a heading to be joined together so that the computer can treat them as one word, and this character is the one usually used.)

What is a record?

A record is a complete unit of related data items organised in named fields.

In our example, the information held on each person seeking a job is stored in a separate record. The third record in our file holds information on Kevin Maher.

What is a field?

A field is a space for a specified item of information in a record. In our example, 7783924 (a specific item of information) is held in the PHONE_NO field of the fifth record of the file. The content of a field is often referred to as a **data item**.

In summary, a data-base may consist of one or more files. Each file consists of a number of records, and each record comprises a number of fields.

Holding a data-base on computer

In order to hold a data-base on computer, we need a data-base program or **data-base management system** (DBMS). On a microcomputer, this is a program that allows us to store information in a data-base, as well as to edit, organise or retrieve that information.

The data-base program is like our own private librarian, who looks after our data-base and carries out any editing, organising or retrieval requests from us.

We now examine how to set up a data-base on a computer and how we can carry out various activities on the file, under the following headings:

1. Defining the data entry form
2. Entering data into the file
3. Editing the file
4. Searching the file
5. Displaying selected fields

6. Sorting the file
7. Indexing the file
8. Changing the record structure
9. Performing mathematical operations
10. Creating reports

1. Defining the data entry form

Before we enter a new file into our computer data-base, we must define the data entry form.

A data entry form is a screen layout resembling a form that displays only one data record at a time, which makes it easier to enter and edit data.

We must decide the following:

(a) the heading of each field within the record structure, for example NAME, ADDRESS;

(b) the maximum width of each field. The longest address is 16 KILKENNY RD, so we must define a field width of 14 for the ADDRESS field to accommodate this address;

(c) the data type: **alphabetic** (letters only), **numeric** (numbers only), or **alphanumeric** (a combination of letters and numbers). In our example the NAME field is alphabetic, the YEARS field is numeric, and the ADDRESS field is alphanumeric.

We would now give our data-base program the following information about our personnel file:

FIELD	FIELD NAME	FIELD WIDTH	DATA TYPE
1	NAME	9	Alphabetic
2	ADDRESS	15	Alphanumeric
3	PHONE_NO	7	Numeric
4	SEX	1	Alphabetic
5	JOB	10	Alphabetic
6	YEARS	2	Numeric

This is the record structure for the file. The corresponding data entry form is displayed below:

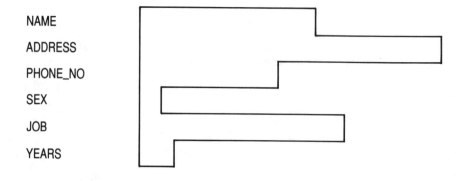

NAME

ADDRESS

PHONE_NO

SEX

JOB

YEARS

2. Entering data into the file

Once we have defined our data entry form, we must now enter data into the file. It is usually entered without punctuation.

It is important that data be entered consistently: in the YEARS field you must not enter '2' in one record and 'two' in the next. This can cause problems when you wish to search or sort the file later. You must take care at this stage, as incorrect data can be entered accidentally.

When you have entered all the data, the file can be displayed on the screen, or printed, and should appear as follows:

NAME	ADDRESS	PHONE_NO	SEX	JOB	YEARS
MURPHY P	6 GREENORE PK	4449234	M	SECRETARY	2
HOPKIRK L	16 KILKENNY RD	8349042	F	SECRETARY	3
MAHER K	56 MAIN ST	8899593	M	CHEF	0
GREENE A	55 WICKLOW RD	5231772	F	ACCOUNTANT	10
BURNS J	57 HAZEL RD	7783924	M	CHEF	2
OWENS M	56 ASHE ST	4931448	F	PHARMACIST	4

3. Editing the file

Once we have set up our file on computer, we can add new records or delete unwanted records. We can also change the contents of individual records in the file.

Adding and deleting records

Let us assume that we have just received the following information about a person who is looking for a job:

Name	Address	Phone	Sex	Job	Years
Aidan McCann	32 Shannon Park	8568264	M	Mechanic	7

We can select the command or option in our data-base program to add a new record to the file. A data entry form appears on the screen, and we simply enter the appropriate details.

Let us also say that Kevin Maher finds a suitable job and no longer requires the agency's services. We can delete his record from the file by using the command or option to delete a record in our data-base program.

The file will now appear as follows:

NAME	ADDRESS	PHONE_NO	SEX	JOB	YEARS
MURPHY P	6 GREENORE PK	4449234	M	SECRETARY	2
HOPKIRK L	16 KILKENNY RD	8349042	F	SECRETARY	3
GREENE A	55 WICKLOW RD	5231772	F	ACCOUNTANT	10
BURNS J	57 HAZEL RD	7783924	M	CHEF	2
OWNES M	56 ASHE ST	4931448	F	PHAMACIST	4
MCCANN A	32 SHANNON PK	8568264	M	MECHANIC	7

Changing the contents of records

Using the appropriate command or option, we can display a record and then delete or insert various items of information.

Let us say that Aisling Greene has moved to 68 Shannon Park, and her new telephone number is 8568234. Also, a mistake was made in the name field of the second record: the name should be Hopkins, not Hopkirk.

When we have made these changes, the file will appear as follows:

NAME	ADDRESS	PHONE_NO	SEX	JOB	YEARS
MURPHY P	6 GREENORE PK	4449234	M	SECRETARY	2
HOPKINS L	16 KILKENNY RD	8349042	F	SECRETARY	3
GREENE A	68 SHANNON PK	8568234	F	ACCOUNTANT	10
BURNS J	57 HAZEL RD	7783924	M	CHEF	2
OWNES M	56 ASHE ST	4931448	F	PHAMACIST	4
MCCANN A	32 SHANNON PK	8568264	M	MECHANIC	7

4. Searching the file

One of the really useful features of having files stored on a computer data-base is the ease and speed with which we can search for information. As records are numbered according to their position in a file, we can cause a particular record to be displayed. We can also display or print all those records that meet a certain condition or set of conditions.

Searching for records by their position in the file

We can select the appropriate command or option to display record 3 in the personnel file:

RECORD NO.	NAME	ADDRESS	PHONE_NO	SEX	JOB	YEARS
3	GREENE A	68 SHANDON PK	8568234	F	ACCOUNTANT	10

Searching for records using one condition

Let us say that Bestmatch Recruitment get a telephone call from a company's personnel officer looking for a secretary. We can search the file for the records containing details of secretaries. We follow these steps:

(*a*) select the option or command for searching the file;

(*b*) choose the correct field for our search: the JOB field;

(*c*) enter the job we are searching for: SECRETARY;

(*d*) some programs may then require the user to give an 'execute' command to start the search.

The results of this search may appear as follows:

NAME	ADDRESS	PHONE_NO	SEX	JOB	YEARS
MURPHY P	6 GREENORE PK	4449234	M	SECRETARY	2
HOPKINS L	16 KILKENNY RD	8349042	F	SECRETARY	3

Searching for records using more than one condition

We can obtain details of those people on our file who are female and who have more than three years' experience in their chosen career, by carrying out the following steps:

(*a*) select the option or command for searching the file;

(*b*) choose the field for our first search condition: the SEX field;

(*c*) enter the sex for which we are searching: FEMALE;

(*d*) choose the field for our second search condition: the YEARS field;

(*e*) select the greater-than operand (>) and enter 3;

(*f*) some programs may then require the user to give an 'execute' command to start the search.

Once the request has been carried out, the results may appear as follows:

NAME	ADDRESS	PHONE_NO	SEX	JOB	YEARS
GREENE A	68 SHANNON PK	8568234	F	ACCOUNTANT	10
OWENS M	56 ASHE ST	4931448	F	PHARMACIST	4

Searching for records using variable symbols

Sometimes we may have to search a file without knowing the precise conditions under which we are performing the search. This can be done by using **variable symbols** (sometimes called 'wild cards'). These are characters (for example ? or *) that the program interprets as 'any character'.

Let us say that someone whose details are on the personnel file has just phoned the agency. The receptionist takes the caller's telephone number and assures her that the manager will return the call within the hour. The manager, however, loses the telephone number, but remembers the first three digits: 834. The data-base program will allow him to search the file for the details of any person whose telephone number starts with 834.

The steps taken to carry out this type of search on most data-base programs are as follows:

(a) select the option or command for searching the file;

(b) choose the correct field for the search: the PHONE_NO field;

(c) enter the portion of the data entry that we know: 834;

(d) fill the remainder of the field with the variable symbol: ****;

(e) some programs may then require the user to give an 'execute' command to start the search.

The result of this search on the personnel file will be displayed as follows:

HOPKINS L	16 KILKENNY RD	8349042	F	SECRETARY	3

5. Displaying selected fields

Another feature of a data-base program is its ability to display only a certain number of fields. This is useful when our records contain a large number of fields.

We may wish to display only the NAME, JOB and YEARS fields of all the records in the file. These are the steps we take:

(a)   select the option or command that enables us to select the fields that we want displayed;

(b)   select the fields in the order in which we would like them displayed;

(c)   then select the command or option to execute the 'display selected fields' facility.

The result should appear as follows:

NAME	JOB	YEARS
MURPHY P	SECRETARY	2
HOPKINS L	SECRETARY	3
GREENE A	ACCOUNTANT	10
BURNS J	CHEF	2
OWENS M	PHARMACIST	4
MCCANN A	MECHANIC	7

It is possible to combine the 'display selected fields' and search facilities.

We may wish to display the NAME, ADDRESS and JOB fields of all those records belonging to the males on file. In order to carry this out we must:

(a) select the fields to be displayed: NAME, ADDRESS, and JOB;

(b) select the option or command for searching the file;

(c) choose the field for the search condition: the SEX field;

(d) enter the sex for which we are searching: MALE;

(e) some programs may then require the user to give an 'execute' command to start the search.

The result should appear as follows:

NAME	ADDRESS	JOB
MURPHY P	6 GREENORE PK	SECRETARY
BURNS J	57 HAZEL RD	CHEF
MCCANN A	32 SHANNON PK	MECHANIC

6. Sorting the file

Another useful feature of our computer data-base is the ease with which we can sort the records. In this section we examine the following methods:

- alphabetic sorting
- numeric sorting
- reverse sorting
- multi-level sorting
- group sorting

Most data-base programs would normally allow us to sort a file in the following way:

(a) select the option or command for sorting;

(b) select the **key field** (this is a field chosen by the user on which sorting will be carried out);

(c) use the option or command to choose whether we wish to sort the records in **ascending order** (with text this is the same as alphabetical order) or descending order. The default setting in most data-base programs is ascending order.

Alphabetical sorting

Let us assume that we wish to sort the records by name, in alphabetical order. The NAME field will thus be the key field. The results of this sort may be displayed as:

NAME	ADDRESS	PHONE_NO	SEX	JOB	YEARS
BURNS J	57 HAZEL RD	7783924	M	CHEF	2
GREENE A	68 SHANNON PK	8568234	F	ACCOUNTANT	10
HOPKINS L	16 KILKENNY RD	8349042	F	SECRETARY	3
MCCANN A	32 SHANNON PK	8568264	M	MECHANIC	7
MURPHY P	6 GREENORE PK	4449234	M	SECRETARY	2
OWENS M	56 ASHE ST	4931448	F	PHARMACIST	4

Numeric sorting

We can sort the file by number of years' job experience of each person. The YEARS field will be chosen as the key field. The sorted file will then appear as follows:

NAME	ADDRESS	PHONE_NO	SEX	JOB	YEARS
MURPHY P	6 GREENORE PK	4449234	M	SECRETARY	2
BURNS J	57 HAZEL RD	7783924	M	CHEF	2
HOPKINS L	16 KILKENNY RD	8349042	F	SECRETARY	3
OWENS M	56 ASHE ST	4931448	F	PHARMACIST	4
MCCANN A	32 SHANNON PK	8568264	M	MECHANIC	7
GREENE A	68 SHANNON PK	8568234	F	ACCOUNTANT	10

Reverse sorting

The file, as it appears above, is sorted in ascending order of number of years' job experience of each person. We can also sort the file in *descending* order, again using the YEARS field as the key field. The sorted file will now appear as:

NAME	ADDRESS	PHONE_NO	SEX	JOB	YEARS
GREENE A	68 SHANNON PK	8568234	F	ACCOUNTANT	10
MCCANN A	32 SHANNON PK	8568264	M	MECHANIC	7
OWENS M	56 ASHE ST	4931448	F	PHARMACIST	4
HOPKINS L	16 KILKENNY RD	8349042	F	SECRETARY	3
MURPHY P	6 GREENORE PK	4449234	M	SECRETARY	2
BURNS J	57 HAZEL RD	7783924	M	CHEF	2

Multi-level sorting

In our examples we have been sorting on one field: either the NAME field or the AGE field. It is possible, however, to sort on a number of fields at the same time.

If we are sorting on two fields, the first field we select is the **primary sort field** and the second is the **secondary sort field**. We can now sort our file using the SEX field as the primary key field and the NAME field as the secondary key field. The result would be as follows:

NAME	ADDRESS	PHONE_NO	SEX	JOB	YEARS
GREENE A	68 SHANDON PK	8568234	F	ACCOUNTANT	10
HOPKINS L	16 KILKENNY RD	8349042	F	SECRETARY	3
OWENS M	56 ASHE ST	4931448	F	PHARMACIST	4
BURNS J	57 HAZEL RD	7783924	M	CHEF	2
MCCANN A	32 SHANNON PK	8568264	M	MECHANIC	7
MURPHY P	6 GREENORE PK	4449234	M	SECRETARY	2

As F comes before M in the alphabet, all the female entries are listed first, in alphabetical order, then the male entries in alphabetical order.

Group sorting

We can select a particular group of records from the file and display this group sorted on one or more fields. We may wish to have all records of those people who have more than two years' experience sorted alphabetically by name, and then displayed.

Some data-base programs may allow us to sort the file using the NAME field as the key field and then search the sorted file for all those people with more than two years' experience. Other programs may allow us to extract the records of those people with more than two years' experience and then sort these records into alphabetical order. The result, in either case, should appear as follows:

NAME	ADDRESS	PHONE_NO	SEX	JOB	YEARS
GREENE A	68 SHANNON PK	8568234	F	ACCOUNTANT	10
HOPKINS L	16 KILKENNY RD	8349042	F	SECRETARY	3
MCCANN A	32 SHANNON PK	8568264	M	MECHANIC	7
OWENS M	56 ASHE ST	4931448	F	PHARMACIST	4

7. Indexing the file

When we sort a data-base file, the records are physically sorted by the computer into the order required. We have seen, in an earlier example, that the records are numbered according to their position in the file.

We can get a print-out of the file sorted on the NAME field:

RECORD NO	NAME	ADDRESS	PHONE_NO	SEX	JOB	YEARS
1	BURNS J	57 HAZEL RD	7783924	M	CHEF	2
2	GREENE A	68 SHANNON PK	8568234	F	ACCOUNTANT	10
3	HOPKINS L	16 KILKENNY RD	8349042	F	SECRETARY	3
4	MCCANN A	32 SHANNON PK	8568264	M	MECHANIC	7
5	MURPHY P	6 GREENORE PK	4449234	M	SECRETARY	2
6	OWENS M	56 ASHE ST	4931448	F	PHARMACIST	4

Many computer data-base programs offer an alternative to sorting, namely **indexing**. We can get a computer print-out of our unsorted file:

RECORD NO	NAME	ADDRESS	PHONE_NO	SEX	JOB	YEARS
1	MURPHY P	6 GREENORE PK	4449234	M	SECRETARY	2
2	HOPKINS L	16 KILKENNY RD	8349042	F	SECRETARY	3
3	GREENE A	68 SHANNON PK	8568234	F	ACCOUNTANT	10
4	BURNS J	57 HAZEL RD	7783924	M	CHEF	2
5	OWENS M	56 ASHE ST	4931448	F	PHARMACIST	4
6	MCCANN A	32 SHANNON PK	8568264	M	MECHANIC	7

If we index our file using the NAME field, the records themselves are not ordered. Instead, the numbers of the records are ordered in a small file called an 'index file'. As BURNS would head the list in alphabetical order, the first number in the index file would be 4, because this person's record is the fourth record in the file. The index file in this case would contain the following list of numbers: 4, 3, 2, 1, 6, 5.

When we activate this index file and then request a print-out, we would obtain the following:

RECORD NO.	NAME	ADDRESS	PHONE_NO	SEX	JOB	YEARS
4	BURNS J	57 HAZEL RD	7783924	M	CHEF	2
3	GREENE A	68 SHANNON PK	8568234	F	ACCOUNTANT	10
2	HOPKINS L	16 KILKENNY RD	8349042	F	SECRETARY	3
6	MCCANN A	32 SHANNON PK	8568264	M	MECHANIC	7
1	MURPHY P	6 GREENORE PK	4449234	M	SECRETARY	2
5	OWENS M	56 ASHE ST	4931448	F	PHARMACIST	4

The records are printed according to the order of the numbers in the index file.

Frequent data-base users rarely use sorting and prefer indexing, as index files can be activated very quickly. Sorting a large file can take some time.

Another advantage of using the indexing rather than sorting facility is that some data-base programs, when sorting a file, set up a completely new file, and copy the records across to this new file in sorted order. We would then have two files containing exactly the same information stored on our disk—one sorted and one unsorted. In this case indexing is obviously preferable to sorting, as index files will take up a much smaller amount of disk space than sort files. The indexing facility is not available on all data-base programs.

8. Changing the record structure

Sometimes, after we have defined the record structure of a file and entered information into it, we may wish to change the record structure. This could be for one or more of the following purposes:

- adding a new field
- deleting an existing field
- changing the order of fields
- widening fields
- changing field names

The commands and techniques to change the record structure vary, depending on the data-base program you are using. As you proceed through this section you should check the appropriate command or technique to undertake a particular change to the record structure.

Changing the field width

The field width of the NAME field in our example was set at 9 in order to accommodate the longest name, which was HOPKIRK L. The field is not wide enough, however, to allow us to include the first names. If we include the first name instead of the initial, Aisling Greene has the longest name: we need a field width of 14 to accommodate this woman's name.

When we have redefined the field width of the NAME field to 14 and edited the file to include the first names, it will appear as follows:

NAME	ADDRESS	PHONE_NO	SEX	JOB	YEARS
BURNS JOHN	57 HAZEL RD	7783924	M	CHEF	2
GREENE AISLING	68 SHANNON PK	8568234	F	ACCOUNTANT	10
HOPKINS LIZ	6 KILKENNY RD	8349042	F	SECRETARY	3
MCCANN AIDAN	32 SHANNON PK	8568264	M	MECHANIC	7
MURPHY DANIEL	6 GREENORE PK	4449234	M	SECRETARY	2
OWENS MARY	56 ASHE ST	4931448	F	PHARMACIST	4

Deleting a field from the record structure

As we have the telephone number of each person on file, there is little need for a field that includes the address. We will use the commands specific to our data-base program to delete this field from the record structure. The file may then appear as follows:

NAME	PHONE_NO	SEX	JOB	YEARS
BURNS JOHN	7783924	M	CHEF	2
GREENE AISLING	8568234	F	ACCOUNTANT	10
HOPKINS LIZ	8349042	F	SECRETARY	3
MCCANN AIDAN	8568264	M	MECHANIC	7
MURPHY DANIEL	4449234	M	MECHANIC	7
OWENS MARY	4931448	F	PHARMACIST	4

Adding a new field to the record structure

As companies often phone the agency from various towns looking for staff in their own area, we might include a TOWN field for the home town of each person on file. When we have set up this new field and included the appropriate details, our file would appear as follows:

NAME	TOWN	PHONE_NO	SEX	JOB	YEARS
BURNS JOHN	TRIM	7783924	M	CHEF	2
GREENE AISLING	NAVAN	8568234	F	ACCOUNTANT	10
HOPKINS LI Z	DROICHEAD NUA	8349042	F	SECRETARY	3
MCCANN AIDAN	MONAGHAN	8568264	M	MECHANIC	7
MURPHY DANIEL	CAVAN	4449234	M	SECRETARY	2
OWENS MARY	TRALEE	4931448	F	PHARMACIST	4

Changing a field name

We can change the name of the field that includes each person's occupation from JOB to CAREER.

Changing the order of fields

We may wish to move the YEARS field so that it appears second in the record structure.

When we have made these final two changes to our record structure, our personnel file will now appear as follows:

NAME	YEARS	TOWN	PHONE_NO	SEX	CAREER
BURNS JOHN	2	TRIM	7783924	M	CHEF
GREENE AISLING	4	NAVAN	8568234	10	ACCOUNTANT
HOPKINS LIZ	3	DROICHEAD NUA	8349042	F	SECRETARY
MCCANN AIDAN	7	MONAGHAN	8568264	M	MECHANIC
MURPHY DANIEL	2	CAVAN	4449234	M	SECRETARY
OWENS MARY	4	TRALEE	4931448	F	PHARMACIST

Careful planning

The facilities for changing a record's structure are very useful but should be used sparingly. A prudent data-base user will always plan the record structure of a new file on paper before defining it on computer. A little early planning with field names and field widths will save a lot of alterations in record structure later.

9. Performing mathematical operations

Two useful facilities offered by most data-base programs are:

(*a*) the ability to perform one of the four basic mathematical operations (add, subtract, multiply, or divide) on the data items of two or more numeric fields and to place the result in another field;

(*b*) the summation function.

Performing mathematical operations on data items

Set up the following file on your computer. It contains details of goods that are for sale at Jim's Electrical Superstore. The file consists of five records, and each record has four fields:

ITEM: the name of the electrical item;

COST: its cost price;

QUANTITY: the number in stock;

RETAIL: its retail price.

The file's contents are as follows:

ITEM	COST	QUANTITY	RETAIL
WASHING MACHINE	250.00	7	318.00
REFRIGERATOR	400.00	3	625.00
VIDEO RECORDER	290.00	8	428.00
TELEVISION	350.00	4	520.00
VACUUM CLEANER	180.00	2	245.00

We can quite easily change the record structure to include two new fields:

PROFIT: the data item in this field will be the profit obtained on the sale of one item, and can be obtained by the simple formula 'retail minus cost', which subtracts the contents of the COST field from the contents of the RETAIL field for each of the five records;

VALUATION: the data item in this field will be the total value of all the items of a particular type, for example the total value of all television sets. The valuation is obtained by a formula, 'cost multiplied by quantity', which multiplies the contents of the COST field by the contents of the QUANTITY field for each of the five records.

When you have set up the file containing the two new fields, it should look like this:

ITEM	COST	QUANTITY	RETAIL	PROFIT	VALUATION
WASHING MACHINE	250.00	7	318.00	68.00	1750.00
REFRIGERATOR	400.00	3	625.00	225.00	1200.00
VIDEO RECORDER	290.00	8	428.00	138.00	2320.00
TELEVISION	350.00	4	520.00	170.00	1400.00
VACUUM CLEANER	180.00	2	245.00	65.00	360.00

The summation function

Most data-base programs have a summation function, which allows us to sum fields. Let us say that someone wishes to buy all five of the items listed in the file. We can use the summation function to obtain the total value of the data items in the RETAIL fields of the five records. We get:

5 records summed on the RETAIL field
Total = £2,136.00

As we will see in the next section, the summation of fields can be carried out automatically when we generate reports.

10. Creating reports

A report is any meaningful information retrieved from a data-base and displayed or printed.

Strictly speaking, all the output from the two files outlined in this chapter are reports. Most data-base programs, however, are equipped with a **report generator.** This is a facility that allows us to design the presentation of the output from a data-base file. The report generator can also total columns of numeric data automatically.

The following is a print-out of a report generated on the electrical shop file:

JIM'S ELECTRICAL SUPERSTORE VALUATION REPORT

ITEM	COST	QUANTITY	RETAIL	PROFIT	VALUATION
WASHING MACHINE	250.00	7	318.00	68.00	1750.00
REFRIGERATOR	400.00	3	625.00	225.00	1200.00
VIDEO RECORDER	290.00	8	428.00	138.00	2320.00
TELEVISION	350.00	4	520.00	170.00	1400.00
VACUUM CLEANER	180.00	2	245.00	65.00	360.00
TOTAL		24			7030.00

Summary

In this chapter we have examined the main facilities of a data-base program. Most of these facilities should be available on your program.

We have dealt with the simplest type of data-base, the **flat-file** data-base. This is one where all the files are treated individually by the program and are not linked in any way. In chapter 4 we will look at other types of data-bases that are in use at the present time.

You are now advised to attempt the assignments in the following chapter.

Chapter 3

Practical data-base assignments

These assignments are graded, and we advise that you work through them in the order in which they are given.

Functions and commands required

As you progress through these assignments you will need to check the functions and commands specific to your data-base program. You will also be practising commands and functions learned in earlier assignments. (*Note*: If you have not got access to a printer, you can display the result of that task instead.)

The functions and commands required for each assignment are as follows:

ASSIGNMENT 1
- Creating a file
- Designing the data entry form
- Entering data
- Editing the contents of individual records
- Adding new records
- Erasing existing records
- Saving and printing a file

ASSIGNMENT 2
Consolidation assignment

ASSIGNMENT 3
Consolidation assignment

ASSIGNMENT 4
- Displaying one record by its position in the file
- Searching on one condition

ASSIGNMENT 5
- Searching on two conditions

ASSIGNMENT 6
- Displaying a record by its position in the file
- Searching on one, two and three conditions
- Displaying selected fields for all the records

ASSIGNMENT 7
- Searching on one, two and three conditions
- Displaying selected fields for all the records
- Combining the 'displaying selected fields' facility with a one-condition search
- Combining the 'displaying selected fields' facility with a two-condition search

ASSIGNMENT 8
- Searching on four conditions
- Combining the 'displaying selected fields' facility with a three-condition search
- Sorting a file in alphabetical order on one field

ASSIGNMENT 9
- Combining the 'displaying selected fields' facility with a four-condition search
- Sorting a file in numerical order on one field (ascending and descending)
- Search a sorted file on one condition
- Researching information and including it in a file
- Indexing a file

ASSIGNMENT 10
Consolidation assignment

ASSIGNMENT 11
- Transferring data from source documents to a data-base file

ASSIGNMENT 12
- Transferring data from source documents to a data-base file
- Altering the record structure: inserting a new field into the existing structure and lengthening a field

ASSIGNMENT 13
- Combining the contents of two manual files into one computer data-base file
- Commands for saving, searching, sorting, and printing
- Finding the averages and totals of common fields over a range of records
- Multiplying the contents of one field by the contents of another field and depositing the result in a new field ('field derivation')

ASSIGNMENT 14
- Transferring data from source documents to a data-base file
- Commands for saving, searching, sorting and printing a file
- Finding the average of a certain field over a group of records

ASSIGNMENT 15
- Transferring data from source documents to a data-base file
- Commands for saving, searching, sorting and printing a file
- Researching information and including it in the file

ASSIGNMENT 1

You are required to set up a file containing information on ten students. The information on each student falls under the following six headings: name, age, sex, telephone number, area, and class.

In data-base language you must set up a file of ten records, each record consisting of six fields. When defining the record structure, the field width for each field is as follows:

Field name	Width
Name	10
Age	2
Sex	1
Phone	7
Area	11
Class	3

Once you have set up your record structure, you should enter the following information into the file:

Name	Age	Sex	Phone	Area	Class
Murphy J	17	M	5612431	Ballsbridge	CB1
Allen P	16	F	8926143	Goatstown	CDN
Timmins R	18	F	8943162	Ballinteer	CB2
Owens A	17	F	8936141	Rathfarnham	CDN
Murphy B	19	M	5612431	Ballsbridge	CDN
Baker M	18	M	3884826	Terenure	CB1
Wilson D	19	F	7317261	Drumcondra	CB2
Cahill M	16	F	5412623	Clontarf	CB2
Dolan S	18	M	4511136	Crumlin	CDN
Dolan P	16	F	4581623	Terenure	CB1

Carry out the following tasks:

Display:

[1] all the details on each student in the file.

Make the following alterations to the relevant records:

[2] P. Allen is male and lives in Churchtown.

[3] M. Cahill is 17 years old.

[4] S. Dolan is a student in CB1 and not CDN.

Delete:

[5] A. Owens's record from the file.

Add:

[6] the following information on a new student who has just joined the school: C. Rahilly, 16, male, 9564338, Drimnagh, CB2.

Print:

[7] this edited version of the file.

ASSIGNMENT 2

A travel agent has the following travel information about fifteen flights written in her log book:

From	Departure	To	Arrival	Time taken	Carrier	Seats left	Cost
Dublin	10:50	London	11:50	1.0	Aer Lingus	32	73
London	13:30	Jerusalem	19:30	3.0	BA	12	155
Manchester	09:00	San Francisco	11:00	10.0	Pan Am	2	480
New York	18:00	London	05:30	6.5	TWA	0	315
Glasgow	14:00	Dublin	15:00	1.0	BA	14	65
Milan	11:00	Manchester	12:30	2.5	Alitalia	0	140
London	10:00	Singapore	05:00	9.0	Qantas	0	450
Shannon	17:30	London	18:30	1.0	Aer Lingus	4	80
Paris	15:00	London	15:00	1.0	Air France	11	85
Luton	17:00	Amsterdam	19:00	1.0	KLM	2	85
Los Angeles	09:00	Manchester	03:00	10.0	Pan Am	0	480
Rome	10:00	London	11:00	2.0	Alitalia	0	135
Moscow	12:00	Luton	11:30	2.5	Aeroflot	0	165
London	22:00	Glasgow	23:00	1.0	BA	6	55
Leeds	15:00	Belfast	16.00	1.0	BA	13	55

You are required to transfer this information to a data-base file on your computer. The record structure for the file is as follows:

Field	Field name	Width
1	FROM	14
2	DEPARTURE	5
3	TO	13
4	ARRIVAL	5
5	TIME_TAKEN	4
6	AIRLINE	10
7	SEATS_LEFT	3
8	COST	3

Carry out the following tasks:

Make the following alterations to the relevant records:

[1] The cost of travelling from Milan to Manchester has been increased to £160.

[2] The flight from Shannon to London, scheduled for 17:30, has been delayed for two hours. Make the appropriate changes to the departure and arrival times.

[3] Amsterdam airport is fog-bound. The flight from Luton has been diverted to Brussels. The expected time of arrival in Brussels is 19:30. Amend the appropriate fields with this information.

[4] The plane due to leave Paris at 15:00 for London has engine problems. The carrier for this flight will now be British Airways, and the flight will depart an hour late. Amend the appropriate fields to reflect these changes.

[5] The flight from Glasgow to Dublin has been cancelled until further notice. Erase the information concerning this flight from the file.

[6] Information on another flight must be added to our file. The details are as follows:

From	Departure	To	Arrival	Time taken	Airline	Seats left	Cost
London	12:00	Bonn	15:00	2.0	BA	18	90.00

Print:

[7] this edited version of the file.

ASSIGNMENT 3

The following is a list of information on twenty films that are available at a nearby video library:

Title	Rating	Type	Leading role	Year	Length	Cert.	Price
My Left Foot	****	Drama (true story)	Daniel Day-Lewis	1989	103	12	2.50
All Dogs Go to Heaven	***	Cartoon	—	1989	88	Gen.	1.50
Sea of Love	****	Romantic thriller	Ellen Barkin	1989	93	18	2.50
The Lady with a Lamp	***	Drama	Anna Neagle	1951	85	12	1.00
Love Story	**	Romantic drama	Ali McGraw	1970	91	12	1.50
The Shining	**	Horror	Jack Nicholson	1980	110	18	2.00
Back to the Future	***	Sci-fi comedy	Michael J. Fox	1985	108	Gen.	2.50
Chariots of Fire	****	Drama (true story)	Ben Cross	1981	102	Gen.	2.00
The Young Philadelphians	***	Drama	Paul Newman	1959	101	12	1.00
Rebel Without a Cause	****	Drama	James Dean	1955	99	15	1.00
Jaws	***	Thriller	Roy Scheider	1975	102	15	1.50
The Goodbye Girl	***	Romance	Richard Dreyfuss	1977	99	15	2.00
The Graduate	****	Satire	Dustin Hoffman	1967	100	18	1.50
The Rainmaker	***	Drama	Burt Lancaster	1956	121	Gen.	1.00
Crimes and Misdemeanors	***	Comedy	Woody Allen	1990	93	15	2.00
Superman	***	Science fiction	Christopher Reeve	1978	143	Gen.	2.00
Batman	***	Science fiction	Michael Keaton	1989	126	12	1.50
The Grapes of Wrath	****	Drama	Henry Fonda	1940	129	Gen.	1.00
Bad Day at Black Rock	****	Drama	Spencer Tracy	1955	81	Gen.	1.00
Dick Tracy	**	Thriller	Warren Beatty	1990	134	12	2.00

The information on each film includes its title, a rating, type, leading actor, year of release, running time, suitability certificate, and cost of hiring.

You are required to set up a data-base file on your computer containing the information on the given films. You can use the column headings given above as field names; you must, however, decide the field lengths and the data type in each field yourself.

Carry out the following tasks:

Print:

[1] the entire file.

Make the following alterations to the relevant records:

[2] The leading role in *Sea of Love* was played by Al Pacino.

[3] *Crimes and Misdemeanors* would be better described as a satire.

[4] *Dick Tracy* should have a three-star rating.

[5] The running time for *The Goodbye Girl* is 104 minutes.

[6] The cost of hiring *All Dogs Go to Heaven* is £2.00.

[7] The video library have withdrawn *The Lady with a Lamp*. Erase the record on this film from the file.

[8] Add the following information on two more films:

Title	Rating	Type	Leading role	Year	Length	Cert.	Price
Ghostbusters	***	Sci-fi comedy	Bill Murray	1984	107	12	£2.00
Dead Poets Society	***	Drama	Robin Williams	1989	128	15	£2.00

Print:

[9] this edited version of the file.

ASSIGNMENT 4

A university welfare officer keeps a file of information on suitable accommodation for the benefit of all first-year students.

The file consists of the name, address and telephone number of people providing suitable accommodation, together with the number of lodging days per week, whether an evening meal is included, the weekly cost, and, most importantly, the availability. The details are as follows:

Name	Address	Telephone	Days	Eve. meal	Cost	Available
Murphy T	6 Beech Road	7894583	5	Yes	32	No
Timmins A	62 Mountain Road	3849332	7	Yes	45	Yes
Burke N	45 Glenmore Avenue	8903393	7	Yes	42	Yes
Lynch H	6 Killarney Road	5943245	7	Yes	45	No
Taylor R	41 Sarsfield Avenue	8343429	7	No	28	No
Phillips E	19 Shandon Avenue	7893632	7	Yes	48	No
Rahilly H	5 Tara Crescent	3849234	5	Yes	30	No
McLoughlin R	23 Goldsmith Place	8903847	7	Yes	40	Yes
Downes S	62 Kilshane Drive	3847828	7	No	28	Yes
Foley G	7 Ivy Road	8574788	7	Yes	42	No
Shiels L	76 Yeats Drive	7893242	7	Yes	40	Yes
Byrne M	6 Brickfield Road	5940202	5	No	25	Yes
Graham M	7 Aughrim Terrace	3849876	7	Yes	42	Yes
Murray C	8 Tara Crescent	3849239	7	Yes	45	No
Wilson F	47 Killowen Gardens	3847872	7	Yes	42	No
Kennedy J	82 Seaview Road	8578398	5	Yes	34	No
Crowley D	61 College Road	8573426	7	Yes	45	Yes
Byrne A	72 Cathedral Place	5949929	7	No	32	Yes
Hanrahan A	46 Fitzgerald Crescent	7893726	7	Yes	42	No
Peterson Y	43 College Road	8573526	5	Yes	34	Yes

You are required to set up a data-base file on your computer and enter the above information into it.

Carry out the following tasks:

Print:

[1] the entire file.

Make the following alterations to the relevant records:

[2] Niamh Burke has just got married. As she will be spending weekends at her husband's country cottage, she cannot keep students at weekends. She has decided to charge £30 for five days' accommodation.

[3] Elizabeth Phillips has just informed the office that the Australian student lodging with her found university life too demanding and has returned to Australia, and Elizabeth can now accommodate one more student.

[4] Sheila Downes has finished taking evening classes and has decided to provide an evening meal for the three students staying at her home, for an additional £12 each per week.

[5] A new motorway is being built near the university, and will pass through Tara Crescent, and the county council has purchased all the houses on this road. All the residents have bought houses in other areas, and the students staying with families on this road have found accommodation elsewhere.

[6] Róisín McLoughlin's neighbour, Deirdre Collins, who lives at no. 22, has just decided to keep students. Her telephone number is 8903842. Enter these details into a new record. The details for the other fields in the record are precisely the same as those in Róisín's record.

Print:

[7] this edited version of the file.

Display:

[8] the seventh record in the file.

Solve the following problem:

[9] A parent has lost the name and address of her daughter's lodgings. She has, however, the telephone number: 8578398. Use the number to find and display all the details of her daughter's accommodation.

ASSIGNMENT 5

A hotelier who specialises in angling holidays has compiled information for her guests on all the lakes within a radius of 10 km of her hotel. She can give the name of any lake, its distance from the hotel, its dominant fish type, other fish in its waters, the availability of boats, the year it was last restocked with young fish, its depth, and its floor type.

The information available is as follows:

Lake	Distance	Dominant fish	Other fish	Boat hire	Restocked	Lake depth	Lake floor
Tully	4.0	Pike	Perch, eel, bream	No	1989	10.2	Sand
Gulladoo	3.4	Pike	Perch, trout, bream	Yes	1988	13.5	Sand
Carrigallen	0.5	Bream	Perch, tench, pike	Yes	1990	8.5	Mud
Cullies	4.2	Bream	Perch, eel, pike	Yes	1990	11.2	Mud
Errew	3.6	Pike	Perch, bream, trout	No	1989	12.8	Sand
Gortamone	11.3	Perch	Bream, eel, pike	No	1987	8.8	Mud
Keeldra	6.4	Pike	Perch, trout	Yes	1988	9.6	Sand
Garadice	7.8	Pike	Perch, trout, eel	Yes	1990	15.4	Sand
Gangin	0.4	Bream	Perch, eel	No	1986	7.6	Mud
Rockfield	3.3	Perch	Pike, eel, bream	Yes	1990	12.1	Sand
Lochnabac	5.6	Trout	Perch, pike	Yes	1989	13.7	Sand
Mosey	0.3	Bream	Perch, pike, eel	No	1986	8.2	Mud
Woodford	4.6	Bream	Perch, eel	No	1987	11.9	Mud
Glasshouse	2.6	Trout	Perch, pike	Yes	1990	10.3	Sand
Killegar	3.2	Perch	Bream, eel, pike	No	1988	9.6	Mud

You are required to set up a data-base file on your computer containing the above information, using the headings given above as field names. You are not given the width of each field or the data type of each field (alphabetic, numeric, or alphanumeric): you must decide the maximum field width and the data type yourself from the information to be entered in the file.

Carry out the following tasks:

Print:

[1] the entire file.

Make the following alterations to the relevant records:

[2] The distance from the hotel to Rockfield Lake, as given in the file, is by an old unapproved road. The distance from the hotel to this lake by the new road is 4.1 km, and this distance should be given in the file.

[3] The dominant fish type in Mosey Lake is perch. Bream should be classified as one of the other fish types available.

[4] Boat hire is available on both Tully and Woodford Lakes.

[5] Lochnabac was restocked with young fish in 1990.

[6] The maximum depth of Garadice Lake has been measured incorrectly. Members of a visiting sub-aqua club have discovered an underwater channel with a depth of 24.3 m, and this must now be reflected in the file as the maximum depth of this lake.

[7] Gortamone lake is 11.3 km from the hotel and should not be listed. Erase this record from the file.

[8] The hotelier, when compiling the information, overlooked an excellent trout lake that is only 7.2 km from the hotel. You must include its details in the file. The information is as follows:

Lake	Distance	Dominant fish	Other fish	Boat hire	Restocked	Lake depth	Lake floor
Calloughs	7.2	Trout	Perch, pike	Yes	1990	14.1	Sand

Print:

[9] this edited version of the file.

Display:

[10] the tenth record only in the file.

Display all the details of those lakes—

[11] where trout is the dominant fish type;

[12] that have a lake floor of mud;

[13] that are less than 4 km from the hotel and that have pike as the dominant fish type.

ASSIGNMENT 6

A hairdressing salon keeps a file on its most frequent customers. The details that go to make up each record in the file are the customer's name, address, and telephone number, the stylist who normally attends the customer, most recent style, cost incurred on most recent visit, and the customer's usual beverage.

The file details are as follows:

Name	Address	Telephone	Stylist	Style	Cost	Beverage
Patricia Roche	56 Rockfield Park	7899473	Jean	Perm	20.00	Coffee
Anne Owens	2 Argyle Road	5583584	Aisling	Perm	12.00	Coffee-d
Margaret Duffy	4 Pembroke Drive	5544929	Mary	Colour	25.00	Coffee-d
Rosemary Grehan	47 Ashford Park	4833732	Louise	Cut & blow-dry	7.50	Tea
John Wilson	19 Brookwood Gardens	5994834	Louise	Dry cut	3.00	None
Clíona Harris	13 Hazel Court	5884382	Liam	Perm	25.00	Tea
Claire Brady	48 Slieverue Road	4942384	Jean	Perm	20.00	Coffee-d
Peter Galvin	46 Rockfield Park	7892352	Gráinne	Colour	25.00	Tea
Patricia Colgan	29 Fairfield Drive	4533891	Aisling	Body-wave	18.00	Tea
Tony Byrne	3 Nutley Drive	8847363	Jean	Streaks	15.00	Tea
Mary Wilson	68 Ashpark Road	4833932	Liam	Perm	25.00	Coffee
Jim Price	56 Larkin Street	7934482	Louise	Cut & blow-dry	7.50	None
Caitríona Browne	9 Beachview Park	8549347	Aisling	Highlights	15.50	Coffee
Denise Murray	78 Fairview Road	4533756	Aisling	Streaks	15.50	Tea
Liam Matthews	5 Seapark Terrace	7382947	Liam	Perm	20.00	Coffee
Geraldine Brady	48 Slieverue Road	4942384	Mary	Colour	25.00	None
Seán Rahilly	68 Wicklow Road	5849932	Jean	Streaks	15.00	Coffee-d
Nóirín Woods	79 Argyle Crescent	5583933	Louise	Dry cut	4.00	Coffee-d
Fionnuala Corry	6 Knockmore Road	8493883	Aisling	Perm	25.00	Coffee-d
Susan Keely	65 Greenpark Road	4633275	Mary	Colour	25.00	Tea

You are required to set up a data-base file on your computer and enter the above information into it.

Carry out the following tasks:

Print:

[1] all the details in the file.

Display:

[2] the ninth record in the file.

Display all the details of those customers—

[3] who live at 48 Slieverue Road;

[4] who prefer decaffeinated coffee (coffee-d) on their visits to the salon;

[5] whose style costs more than £20 and who had tea on their last visit;

[6] who were dealt with by Jean and who had streaks put in their hair;

[7] who were attended either by Jean or Liam and who had a perm.

Display:

[8] the NAME, PHONE_NO and STYLIST fields for all customers in the file.

ASSIGNMENT 7

The following information on twenty restaurants is available to all visitors to a certain city from the city tourist board:

Name	Address	Telephone	Open	Close	Food	Category
Zhou's	33 Vine Street	4361735	12:30	01:30	Chinese	Inexpensive
The Stewpot	31 Green Street	3172813	13:00	23:00	Irish	Expensive
Yankee Doodle	43 Greenleaf Way	6412863	11:00	01:00	American	Inexpensive
Luigi's	92 Alley Way	4271132	10:30	02:30	Italian	Moderate
Mangez Bien	115 Vesey Street	1271834	13:00	01:30	French	Expensive
Rosita's	52 Vine Street	4263429	11:00	00:30	Mexican	Expensive
Karto's Kitchen	63 Lombard Grove	2616143	10:00	02:00	Greek	Moderate
Clementine's	8 Fern Road	6163817	13:00	02:00	Fish & chips	Inexpensive
The Inn Place	51 Main Street	6167781	10:00	03:30	American	Inexpensive
Paulo's Pizzas	126 Main Street	6169314	08:30	00:30	Italian	Moderate
Speedy Gonzalez	19 Vine Street	4613381	13:00	02:20	Mexican	Inexpensive
Banjo's Bagels	16 Lee Green	5142681	18:00	23:00	American	Inexpensive
Buena Vista	465 East Wharf	4817261	08:00	01:30	American	Moderate
Mama's Pasta	5 Alley Way	4273166	18:00	03:00	Italian	Expensive
La Belle Ville	36 Lee Green	7181163	18:00	22:00	French	Moderate
Kazmir's Cuisine	96 Alley Way	4271158	18:00	02:30	Indian	Moderate
Home Cookin'	56 Green Street	3815682	08:30	18:00	American	Inexpensive
The Great Wall	41 Vesey Street	1271142	19:00	04:00	Chinese	Moderate
The Khyber Pass	38 Green Street	3172885	18:00	02:00	Indian	Expensive
Oodles of Noodles	91 Main Street	6164371	12:30	00:30	Chinese	Moderate

You are required to set up a data-base file on your computer and to enter this information. In setting up the file you can use the above headings as field names; you must, however, decide for yourself the field width of each field and whether the data to be entered in each field is alphabetic, numeric, or alphanumeric.

Carry out the following tasks:

Display all the details of those restaurants—

[1] that are in the inexpensive category;

[2] that are in the moderate category and serve Chinese food;

[3] that open at 18:00 and close at 22:00;

[4] that open before 11:00 and are categorised as inexpensive and specialise in American food;

[5] that are in the expensive category and serve Italian or Mexican food.

Display:

[6] the name, address, telephone number and type of food served for all the restaurants in the file;

[7] the name, address and telephone number of all the Indian restaurants in the file;

[8] the name, address, telephone number and opening time of any Italian restaurants that are categorised as expensive.

ASSIGNMENT 8

An evening college has begun enrolling for its winter classes. The admissions office has a file that contains the following information:

Title	Department	Code	Day	Time	Wks	Size	Teacher	Exam	Fee
Beauty care	Leisure	GBC	Monday	19:30–20:30	10	18	Louise Saunders	n.a.	17.00.
Mathematics	Mathematics	G3	Monday	19:00–20:30	25	20	John Roche	Leaving Cert.	75.00
Accountancy	Commerce	AC5	Wednesday	19:00–20:00	25	20	Desmond Cox	AAT—paper 6	75.00
Typing—elementary	Secretarial	TY01	Tuesday	19:00–20:30	15	18	Marion Murray	Pitman Elementary	60.00
Typing—intermediate	Secretarial	TY02	Thursday	20:30–22:00	15	18	Helen Redmond	Pitman Intermediate	60.00
Data processing—elementary	Computer	DR01	Monday	19:00–20:30	20	12	Dermot Cahill	CGL 0726/401	80.00
Personnel management	Commerce	PM	Monday	19:00–21:00	20	15	Andrew Dodds	n.a.	46.00
Word-processing—elementary	Computer	WP1	Thursday	19:00–20:30	15	16	James Owens	Pitman Elementary	90.00
Word-processing—intermediate	Computer	WP2	Thursday	20:30–22:00	15	12	Jean Stewart	Pitman Intermediate	90.00
Cobol programming	Computer	CPCG	Wednesday	19:00–21:00	30	15	Susan Farrell	CGL 424	150.00

Aerobics for women	Leisure	AW3	Tuesday	20:00–21:30	10	12	Jenny Smith	n.a.	25.00
Cookery for beginners	Home Economics	HB1	Monday	19:15–21:15	10	15	Laura Elliot	n.a.	35.00
Creative knitting	Home Economics	HC3	Wednesday	19:30–21:30	10	25	Sandra Gregg	n.a.	30.00
Advanced hairdressing	Hairdressing	AHD1	Tuesday	19:00–22:00	15	10	Peter Nicholls	CGL Master Diploma	85.00
Computers for beginners	Computer	CCB	Thursday	19:00–20:30	10	20	Gerry Martin	n.a.	30.00
Programming in Basic	Computer	BS1	Thursday	20:00–22:00	10	15	Stephen Burns	n.a.	40.00
Shorthand	Secretarial	SP	Monday	19:00–21:00	25	20	Mary Andrews	Pitman Elementary	50.00
Bookkeeping	Commerce	BKB	Tuesday	20:00–22:00	10	25	Paul Attley	n.a.	45.00
Spanish for beginners	Languages	SB1	Thursday	19:00–20:00	10	22	Rosita de Santos	n.a.	25.00
Advanced French	Languages	FA3	Wednesday	20:00–21:00	10	22	Pierre Marton	n.a.	25.00
Hotel management	Home Economics	HB7	Tuesday	18:45–21:45	25	12	Leslie Jennings	CGL 491	120.00
Furniture restoration	Home Economics	HC4	Monday	19:30–21:30	10	15	Una Duffy	n.a.	35.00
Business law	Marketing	BLM1	Thursday	18:30–19:30	15	20	Michelle Greene	Cert. in Marketing (1)	60.00
English for non-readers	English	ENNR	Tuesday	20:00–22:00	30	12	Máire Wilson	n.a.	0.00
Yoga	Leisure	YL1	Wednesday	19:00–20:30	10	16	Linda Behan	n.a.	25.00
Business German	Languages	BG4	Monday	20:00–21:30	15	18	Petra Lamvelt	RSA stage 3	85.00
Spreadsheet methods 1	Computer	SM	Wednesday	19:00–20:30	15	15	Matthew Brennan	CGL 726/402	85.00
Microwave cookery	Home Economics	HB4	Wednesday	19:30–21:30	4	15	Una Duffy	n.a.	18.00
Flower arranging	Home Economics	HFA	Tuesday	20.00–22.00	10	12	Anne Nolan	n.a.	30.00
Business administration	Commerce	BA2	Thursday	19:30–20:30	25	22	Michael Moore	AAT level 1	85.00

You are required to transfer these details into a data-base file on your computer. The duration of each course is given in weeks.

Carry out the following tasks:

Print:

[1] the entire file.

Display:

[2] all the details for the course that has the code SP.

Display all the details of those courses—

[3] that will be taught by Una Duffy;

[4] that cost less than £50 and will be taught on Tuesdays;

[5] that are offered by the Computer Department and have a duration of more than fifteen weeks;

[6] that are held from 19:00 to 20:30, have no end-of-course examinations and have class sizes of less than twenty;

[7] that are offered by the Home Economics Department between 19:30 and 21:30 on Wednesday evenings;

[8] that are offered by the Computer Department on Thursdays, have class sizes of less than twenty students and have a duration of less than fifteen weeks.

Display:

[9] the title, day, time and fee for all the courses;

[10] the title, department, teacher, examination and fee of all the courses offered by the Home Economics Department;

[11] the title, department, class size, day, time, duration, teacher and fee (in that order) of all the courses that are planned for Monday or Wednesday;

[12] the title, department, class size, duration, day and fee (in that order) of any course offered by the Hairdressing Department on Tuesdays that has a duration of less than twenty weeks and a class size of less than eighteen.

Print:

[13] the entire file sorted in alphabetical order by course title.

ASSIGNMENT 8

You are required to set up a data-base file containing information on the twenty-two countries listed below. The information includes the name of the country, its area (in square kilometres), population, capital city, and currency unit, the principal language spoken, the annual income per head (in American dollars), and the annual birth rate (per thousand people).

You can use the headings below as field names in setting up the file, but you must establish the field width and data type of each field for yourself.

Carry out the following tasks:

Print:

    [1] the entire file.

Display all the details of those countries—

    [2] that have an annual population growth of between 10 and 30 per thousand;

    [3] that have either Portuguese or Spanish as the principal language and have populations greater than 25 million;

    [4] that have an area less than 200,000 km², a population greater than 80 million, and a birth rate greater than 25 per thousand;

    [5] where English is the principal language, the population is between 20 and 100 million, and the birth rate is less than 12 per thousand.

Display:

    [6] the country, capital city, principal language and annual income of all countries that have an annual income greater than $10,000 per head;

    [7] the country, population, area and annual income per head of all countries that have a population greater than 80 million and an annual income of less than $1,000 per head;

    [8] the country, capital city, population, area, annual income per head and population growth of any country that has an area of less than 100,000 km², a population less than 10 million, and an annual income less than $5,000 per head.

Sort the file—

    [9] into alphabetical order of country name, and display the sorted version of the file on the screen;

    [10] into descending order of annual income, and display the sorted version of the file on the screen;

    [11] into ascending order of annual income, and display all the details of those countries that have English as the principal language from this sorted file.

Research:

    [12] the relevant information for the EC countries that do not appear in the file, and include these details in the file.

Country	Area	Population	Capital city	Currency unit	Principal language	Annual income	Pop. growth
France	551,000	55,300,000	Paris	franc	French	8,850	4
United States	9,372,614	241,000,000	Washington	dollar	English	11,695	9
India	3,166,829	778,520,000	New Delhi	rupee	Hindi	217	21
China	9,596,961	1,050,000,000	Beijing	yuan	Chinese	223	9
Japan	372,313	121,400,000	Tokyo	yen	Japanese	9,684	6
Soviet Union	22,402,200	280,700,000	Moscow	ruble	Russian	3,400	8
Canada	9,976,139	25,650,000	Ottawa	dollar	English	10,275	10
Switzerland	41,293	6,510,000	Bern	franc	German	14,066	2
Saudi Arabia	2,150,000	11,520,000	Riyadh	riyal	Arabic	13,400	30
Australia	7,682,300	15,850,000	Canberra	dollar	English	9,518	13
Britain	229,980	54,940,000	London	pound	English	7,550	1
Ireland	84,421	5,090,000	Dublin	pound	English	4,355	10
Brazil	8,511,965	140,650,000	Brasília	cruzado	Portuguese	2,100	23
Argentina	2,766,889	31,700,000	Buenos Aires	peso	Spanish	2,500	16
Peru	1,285,215	20,000,000	Lima	sol	Spanish	1,010	24
Bangladesh	144,000	104,250,000	Dhaka	taka	Bengali	117	28
Ethiopia	1,221,900	42,580,000	Addis Ababa	birr	Amharic	126	7
Pakistan	803,943	89,831,000	Islamabad	rupee	Urdu	354	30
Nigeria	923,768	94,300,000	Lagos	naira	English	740	34
Kenya	582,646	21,040,000	Nairobi	shilling	Swahili	315	42
Italy	301,225	57,300,000	Rome	lira	Italian	5,512	3
Thailand	514,820	53,700,000	Bangkok	bat	Thai	793	20

Using the indexing facility of your program—

[13] produce a print-out of the entire file, sorted into ascending order of population.

ASSIGNMENT 10

A farmer has twenty cattle for sale. He holds information about each animal in a file. This information consists of each animal's tag number, its age, sex, breed, colour, and weight, whether it was fed milk (natural) or milk replacer (artificial) as a calf, whether the animal has an export permit, which diseases, if any, it has contracted during its life on this farm, and the price the farmer expects to receive from the sale of the animal at the local cattle market.

The details on each animal are as follows:

Tag no.	Age	Sex	Breed	Colour	Weight	Calf feed	Export permit	Disease	Price
FGR85932	2	M	Limousin	Black	360	Natural	Yes	None	680.00
RBH56437	2	F	Friesian	Black-white	350	Natural	Yes	None	800.00
RBH57832	2	M	Friesian	Black-white	385	Natural	No	Blackleg	630.00
YHR65887	3	M	Hereford	Red-white	620	Natural	Yes	None	920.00
FGR63428	2	F	Limousin	Black	320	Artificial	Yes	None	580.00
YHR87445	3	M	Charolais	Buff	660	Natural	Yes	None	975.00
YHR69355	3	M	Simmental	Red	640	Artificial	Yes	None	910.00
RBH77395	3	M	Hereford	Red-white	610	Artificial	No	Ringworm	720.00
FGR69347	2	F	Friesian	Black-white	380	Natural	Yes	None	775.00
YHR46342	3	F	Friesian	Black-white	580	Artificial	Yes	None	995.00
RBH89456	2	M	Charolais	Buff	360	Artificial	Yes	None	680.00
FGR69335	3	F	Hereford	Red-white	550	Artificial	Yes	None	790.00
RBH75669	2	F	Limousin	Black	290	Artificial	Yes	Pinkeye	550.00
PPY59348	3	M	Charolais	Buff	680	Natural	Yes	None	990.00
PPY57889	3	M	Hereford	Black-white	640	Natural	No	None	750.00
FGR69553	2	F	Hereford	Red-white	370	Natural	Yes	None	550.00
RBH68988	2	F	Charolais	Buff	390	Artificial	Yes	None	760.00
YHR55732	3	M	Limousin	Black	490	Artificial	Yes	Red-water	590.00
SDR67738	4	M	Charolais	Buff	920	Natural	Yes	None	930.00
RBH89460	2	F	Friesian	Black-white	410	Natural	Yes	None	860.00

You are required to set up a data-base file on your computer and to enter the information given above.

Carry out the following tasks:

Print:

[1] the entire file.

Make the following alterations to the relevant records:

[2] The farmer has decided to sell two more animals, and these details must be added to the file:

Tag no.	Age	Sex	Breed	Colour	Weight	Calf feed	Export permit	Disease	Price
RBH79942	2	F	Hereford	Red-white	355	Natural	Yes	Hoose	530
FGR25517	2	M	Friesian	Black-white	375	Natural	Yes	None	640

[3] The farmer has decided not to sell the three-year old Friesian with tag number YHR46342: erase the details concerning this animal from the file.

[4] The cattle with the FGR prefix on their tags have to be re-tagged: the new tags have the same numbers but the prefix is now IRE.

Print:

[5] this edited version of the entire file.

Display:

[6] all the details of the three-year old male Charolais cattle that are for sale;

[7] all the details of those cattle that did not succumb to any diseases, that were fed naturally, and now weigh more than 500 kg;

[8] the breed, sex, weight and cost of all Limousin cattle that cost between £600 and £700.

Display (use either the indexing or straight sorting method):

[9] all the details on the Hereford cattle in the file, in ascending order of price;

[10] the age, price, and weight, in descending order of weight, of all the female cattle.

ASSIGNMENT 11

Three dentists have set up a dental clinic together. They presently hold patient information on record cards. A blank card would appear as follows:

Name	**Address**	**Age** ....
Last appt	**Work done**	
Next appt	**Time**	**Med Card** ....
Dentist		

They now wish to hold this patient information on a computer database file. You are required to set up this file on your computer.

Dennis Aherne 06/01/90 04/03/91 Mary Graham	5 Greenore Park 2 Fillings 11:00	22 Yes
Mary Jones 25/03/90 05/03/91 Anne Maher	78 Annamore Road Capping 15:00	17 No
Brendan Morris 12/01/90 04/03/91 Mary Graham	50 Oaktree Road Fillings 10:30	24 No
Carmel Byrne 03/03/90 06/03/91 Mary Graham	3 Balfe Drive Extraction 15:30	42 No
Liam Norris 26/05/90 24/03/91 Anne Maher	42 Galway Square Cleaning 12:30	69 Yes
Angela Maher 06/09/90 04/03/91 Peter Stephenson	4 Shaw Place Bridge 16:00	35 No
Anita Dooley 03/04/90 05/03/91 Peter Stephenson	38 Grangemore Road Extraction 11:00	23 Yes
Emma Norton 19/08/90 06/03/91 Anne Maher	53 Antrim Road Cleaning 14:00	41 Yes
Peter Higgins 23/03/90 07/03/91 Mary Graham	88 Glaslough Park Root canal 13:30	38 No
Linda Burke 16/07/90 14/03/91 Anne Maher	7 Carnbeg Road Fillings 15:00	53 Yes

Paul Halpin 24/04/90 05/03/91 Peter Stephenson	173 Leinster Park Capping 10:30	16 Yes
Stephen Byrne 30/06/90 04/03/91 Mary Graham	39 Oaktree Road Root canal 14:30	25 No
Thomas Roche 02/07/90 05/03/91 Peter Stephenson	12 Highbank Terrace Bridge 16:00	29 No
Mary Noble 15/06/90 20/03/91 Anne Maher	29 Arklow Place Cleaning 16:00	19 No
Siobhán Noble 22/06/90 06/03/91 Peter Stephenson	29 Arklow Place Filling 11:30	21 No
Helen Masterson 16/04/90 06/03/91 Peter Stephenson	27 Grangemore Park Fillings 14:30	54 No
Bernard Brady 19/05/90 22/03/91 Anne Maher	44 Waterford Terrace Cleaning 11:30	73 Yes
Mary Hughes 14/04/90 06/03/91 Peter Stephenson	52 Harbour Place Capping 10:00	42 No
Eithne Kelleher 16/03/90 05/03/91 Mary Graham	13 College Road Extraction 15:30	50 No
Daniel Crowley 14/07/90 06/04/91 Mary Graham	7 Priory Avenue Root canal 12:00	22 No

Carry out the following tasks:

Print:

[1] the entire file.

Make the following alterations to the relevant records:

[2] Mary Jones has moved house and now lives at 23 Kilmore Road.

[3] Anita Dooley was born on 14 June 1965.

[4] Thomas Roche last appeared at the clinic on 3 July 1990, and Anne Maher carried out the required dental work.

[5] Brendan Morris has phoned to cancel his appointment for 4 March; he has been given a new appointment for 16:30 on 7 March.

[6] The ages of the Noble sisters have been transposed, and both women have medical cards.

[7] An inferior cleaning material was used at the clinic during 1990; it has been decided to call back all patients who had their teeth cleaned during that period for a complimentary cleaning on the afternoon of 15 March 1991. The four people concerned should be given appointment times according to the alphabetical order of their names; Anne Maher will see each one for thirty minutes from 14:00 hours.

[8] Make an appointment for yourself on 7 March at 14:00. You last visited the clinic on 14 September 1990, when Mary Graham performed an extraction.

[9] The surname of each patient should appear first in the name field.

Print:

[10] the whole file after the above changes have been carried out.

Display all the details of those patients—

[11] who were attended by Peter Stephenson on their last visit to the clinic;

[12] who had an extraction the last time they attended the clinic;

[13] who are less than twenty-five years old and who do not have a medical card;

[14] who are between twenty and thirty years old and who are normally attended by Mary Graham.

Display:

[15] the name, last appointment date, work done and relevant dentist for all patients who have afternoon appointments for 4 March 1991.

Print:

[16] the entire file sorted into ascending order of age.

ASSIGNMENT

A garage owner has records of used cars for sale contained on sales cards. A blank card looks as follows:

Make	**Type**	**Colour** ....
Year	**County**	**Reg** ....
Price		

The following are records of cars for sale;

Opel	Corsa	Red	
1988	Carlow	88-CW-463	
6,500			

Ford	Escort	Green
1986	Dublin	86-D-48
5,800		

Nissan	Bluebird	White
1989	Longford	89-LD-488
10,600		

Opel	Kadett	Blue
1987	Tipperary	87-TN-789
8,300		

Ford	Orion	White
1987	Dublin	87-D-25800
9,200		

Nissan	Bluebird	Red
1987	Dublin	87-D-18976
10,600		

Toyota	Starlet	Green
1986	Wicklow	86-WW-19
4,800		

Daihatsu	Charade	Red
1989	Meath	89-MH-6705
7,500		

Volkswagen	Golf	Black
1988	Limerick	88-L-9266
8,100		

Toyota	Carina	Blue
1987	Tipperary	87-TN-7893
8,600		

Mazda	626	Black
1988	Kerry	88-KY-200
8,800		

Volkswagen	Passat	Red
1988	Cavan	88-CN-889
11,500		

Toyota	Starlet	Silver
1989	Dublin	89-D-6794
7,800		

Mazda	323	Silver
1990	Galway	90-G-1449
10,200		

Volkswagen	Jetta	Silver
1988	Cork	88-C-7826
8,400		

Fiat	Tipo	Red
1988	Cavan	88-CN-7809
7,200		

Mazda	323	White
1987	Cork	87-C-5676
6,400		

Volkswagen	Golf	White
1984	Galway	84-G-22
3,600		

Ford	Fiesta	Blue
1985	Westmeath	85-WH-11
4,100		

Mazda	323	Red
1988	Donegal	88-DL-1699
7,400		

Volkswagen	Polo	Green
1990	Wexford	90-WX-3488
9,800		

Ford	Sierra	Black
1988	Dublin	88-D-23562
10,300		

Nissan	Micra	Green
1987	Dublin	87-D-4877
6,100		

Volvo	240	Blue
1987	Dublin	87-D-4533
9,800		

Ford	Escort	Silver
1987	Leitrim	87-LM-343
5,800		

Nissan	Micra	Silver
1988	Cork	88-C-8933
7,200		

Rover	Vitesse	Black
1985	Rosc.	85-RN-78
10,200		

Ford	Fiesta	Brown
1988	Mayo	88-MO-980
7,100		

Nissan	Sentra	Blue
1985	Monaghan	85-MN-18
6,300		

Renault	9GTL	Green
1986	Offaly	86-OY-67
8,700		

You are required to set up a file of thirty records on your computer that will contain the above information. Each record will have seven fields: make, type, year, county, colour, registration number, and price.

Carry out the following tasks:

Print:

[1] the entire file.

Make the following alterations to the relevant records:

[2] The 1984 Volkswagen Golf has been re-sprayed using red paint: make the appropriate change to this record.

[3] A new field must be added, for mileage; the details to be included for each record are as follows:

Make	Type	Year	Mileage
Opel	Corsa	1988	57,600
Opel	Kadett	1987	68,900
Toyota	Starlet	1986	86,000
Toyota	Carina	1987	47,800
Toyota	Starlet	1989	14,500
Fiat	Tipo	1988	43,200
Ford	Fiesta	1985	93,000
Ford	Sierra	1988	47,000
Ford	Escort	1987	48,000
Ford	Fiesta	1988	36,000
Ford	Escort	1986	54,000
Ford	Orion	1987	33,600
Daihatsu	Charade	1989	23,000
Mazda	626	1988	35,800
Mazda	323	1990	9,400
Mazda	323	1987	33,400
Mazda	323	1988	28,500
Nissan	Micra	1987	31,600
Nissan	Micra	1988	38,900
Nissan	Sentra	1985	76,400
Nissan	Bluebird	1989	18,000
Nissan	Bluebird	1987	52,300
Volkswagen	Golf	1988	21,700
Volkswagen	Passat	1988	37,800
Volkswagen	Jetta	1988	22,700
Volkswagen	Golf	1984	101,500
Volkswagen	Polo	1990	12,800
Volvo	240	1987	54,000
Rover	Vitesse	1985	67,000
Renault	9GTL	1986	49,500

[4] The mileage of the car registered in Co. Leitrim should be 58,000.

[5] The garage owner wishes to revalue all his Nissan cars and charge a further £200 on each Nissan he has in stock.

[6] The garage has just sold the 1989 Toyota Starlet registered in Co. Dublin.

[7] The following information on three more cars that the garage has bought needs to be added to the file:

Make	Type	Year	County	Colour	Reg.	Price	Mileage
Ford	Escort	1987	Meath	Green	87-MH-5633	6,100	34,700
Volkswagen	Jetta	1989	Clare	Silver	89-CE-455	9,600	15,800
Mitsubishi	Lancer	1989	Sligo	White	89-SO-1892	11,100	12,700

Display:

[8] the seventh record in the file;

[9] the car with the registration number that begins 87-D-48 …

Display all the cars in the file—

[10] that are registered in Co. Dublin;

[11] whose mileage exceeds 60,000;

[12] that were registered in 1988 and now cost less than £8,000;

[13] that are black or white in colour;

[14] that are red in colour and cost between £6,000 and £8,000.

Display:

[15] all the cars in the file, showing only the make, type, year, and price;

[16] the make, type, year, mileage and price of all the Ford cars with a mileage of less than 50,000;

[17] the total income generated by the sale of all the cars on file;

[18] the average cost of a used car sold by this garage;

[19] the average cost of a used Ford car sold by this garage.

Print:

[20] in descending order of price, the make, type, colour, price and registration number of all the cars not manufactured by Nissan or Mazda.

ASSIGNMENT 13

An electrical shop holds two files containing information on all the household applicances it has for sale: a prices file and a stock file. The details in the prices file consist of the item type, the manufacturer, cost price, and retail price.

The information on this file is as follows:

Item	Manufacturer	Cost price	Retail price
Washing machine	Hodges	230.00	299.00
Vacuum cleaner	Mercetron	80.00	104.00
Dishwasher	Lazlo	437.00	568.10
Television	Mercetron	350.00	455.00
Video recorder	Mercetron	242.00	314.60
Television	Ayako	320.00	416.00
Record player	Hyushi	140.00	182.00
Refrigerator	Rodeoking	480.00	624.00
Refrigerator	Ayako	410.00	533.00
Microwave oven	Hodges	120.00	156.00
Jug-kettle	Ayako	8.00	10.40
Coffee maker	Ayako	12.00	15.60
Video recorder	Nanubi	236.00	306.80
Deep-fat fryer	Rodeoking	35.00	45.50
Cassette radio	Hyushi	4.00	5.20

The stock file also contains the name of each item and the manufacturer's name. The other information held on each appliance in this file includes the country of origin, the number of units in stock, and the number of years for which the appliance is under guarantee. The information in this file is as follows:

Item	Manufacturer	Country	Stock	Guarantee
Washing machine	Hodges	Britain	8	4
Vacuum cleaner	Mercetron	Netherlands	11	2
Dishwasher	Lazlo	Italy	62	3
Television	Mercetron	Netherlands	41	5
Video recorder	Mercetron	Netherlands	25	3
Television	Ayako	Japan	12	6
Record player	Hyushi	Japan	26	2
Refrigerator	Rodeoking	United States	53	5
Refrigerator	Ayako	Japan	35	4
Microwave oven	Hodges	Britain	4	3
Jug-kettle	Ayako	Japan	39	1
Coffee maker	Ayako	Japan	21	2
Video recorder	Nanubi	Canada	17	3
Deep-fat fryer	Rodeoking	United States	2	6
Cassette radio	Hyushi	Japan	27	1

You are required to set up one computer data-base file that combines the information given in both of these files.

Carry out the following tasks:

Print:

[1] the entire file.

Display:

[2] the item name, manufacturer and retail price of all the items of Dutch origin.

Alter the record structure—

[3] to include a 'Profit' field. Explore the method of subtracting the contents of the 'Cost price' field from the contents of the 'Retail price' field and depositing the result in the 'Profit' field for each record in the file;

[4] by multiplying the contents of the 'Retail price' field by the contents of the 'Stock' field and depositing the result in a new 'Total retail' field for each record in the file.

Display:

[5] the total number of items in stock;

[6] the total retail value of the shop's stock;

[7] the total number of televisions for sale;

[8] the average cost price of a television set;

[9] the average retail price of a refrigerator;

[10] the name, manufacturer, country of origin, cost price and retail price of all items that have a guarantee of more than three years and are not manufactured in Japan.

Print:

[11] in descending order of retail price, the name, manufacturer and retail price of all the items in the file that are of Japanese origin.

Produce a report—

[12] including the total number of items in stock and the total retail value of all the stock.

ASSIGNMENT 14

Rathcar Computer Supplies Ltd has the following thirty-five computer programs in stock:

Word-processing
Borland Sprint (Borland) **31933** £190
Microsoft Word 5 (Microsoft) **31988** £288
Multimate Advantage 3.6 (Ashton-Tate) **31992** £315
PFS Professional Write (Software Publishing) **32196** £220
Smart with Spell (Informix) **31967** £450
Wordperfect 5 (Wordperfect) **31925** £290
Wordstar Professional 6 (Wordstar) **31903** £285

Document-processing and page make-up
Newsroom (Springboard) **31870** £488
Pagemaker 4 (Aldus) **31945** £580
PFS First Publisher (Software Publishing) **31821** £520
Ventura (Xerox) **31866** £550

Spreadsheets
Borland Quattro (Borland) **31908** £180
Excel 1.5 (Microsoft) **31822** £345
Lotus 1-2-3 (Lotus) **31693** £320
Supercalc 5 (Computer Association) **32116** £318
VP Planner (Paperback Software) **32281** £108

Data-base management
Data Ease (Sapphire Systems) **32004** £320
Dbase III Plus (Ashton-Tate) **31991** £390
Dbase IV (Ashton-Tate) **31995** £440
Paradox (Ansa Software) **32011** £480
Q&A (Symantec) **32020** £180
VP Expert (Paperback Software) **31815** £150

Integrated packages
Ability (Migent) **32217** £170
Ability Plus (Migent) **32221** £215
Framework 3 (Ashton-Tate) **32183** £440
Lotus Symphony (Lotus) **31909** £475
Microsoft Works (Microsoft) **32013** £185

Graphics
Farm Tool (Bloc Development) **32271** £85
Harvard Graphics (Software Publishing) **32167** £355
Mac Paint 1.5 (Claris) **32091** £75
PC-Paintbrush Plus (Z-Soft) **31931** £145

Programming languages
Microsoft C (Microsoft) **32296** £370
Microsoft Macro Assembler (Microsoft) **32281** £145
Turbo Basic (Borland) **31818** £140
Turbo C (Borland) **31956** £180

You are required to set up a data-base file on your computer and to enter the above details. You will have five fields in each record: the type of program (for example word-processor, data-base); the program name; the manufacturer; the code; and the price.

Carry out the following tasks:

Print:

> [1] the entire file.

Display:

> [2] all the details of the program that has the code 32221;

> [3] all the details of the data-base programs only;

> [4] all the details of the language programs that cost less than £150;

> [5] the names, program types and prices of all the software on file produced by Ashton-Tate;

> [6] the name, price and code of all the graphics software on file that costs less than £150;

> [7] the average price of a word-processor program according to the information in the file;

> [8] the program name, manufacturer and code number for all records, sorted in ascending order of code;

> [9] the names and prices of programs manufactured by Borland, sorted in descending order of price.

Print:

> [10] the entire file, sorted in alphabetical order of software name.

ASSIGNMENT 15

Surebet Homefinders is an agency that provides the following services:

(a) for the tenant: finding suitable accommodation at a reasonable rent;

(b) for the property owner: finding suitable tenants.

You have been employed by the agency to set up a computer data-base file of suitable houses for letting from the existing file. Some of the information in the existing file, however, is irrelevant.

Decide, from the information the agency requires in questions 1 to 11 below, the seven most relevant items of information for carrying out this task. The data entry form must contain seven fields, each field containing one of the relevant items of information. It is essential that you define the data entry form on paper before you define it on computer.

The information in the existing file has some special abbreviations:

bed. (bedroom)

/cal.mth (per calendar month)

CH (central heating)

det. (detached)

mod. cons. (modern conveniences)

semi. (semi-detached)

Do not use these abbreviations in entering the information into the data-base file.

The details on the houses in the existing file are as follows:

At Hazel Rd, Blanchardstown—new det. fully furnished house, 4 bed., 600 m from new railway station and same distance from new motorway; first letting; features include en-suite bedroom, south-facing garden, patio doors, and high standard of fit-out, including gas CH; rent £620/cal.mth.

At Iona Rd, Glasnevin—semi., 3 bed., furnished, solid-fuel CH; rent £400/cal.mth.

At Antrim Rd, Rathfarnham—large semi., 4 bed., unfurnished, main bedroom en-suite, oil CH; rent £420/cal.mth.

At Kilmacud Rd, Stillorgan—large semi., 3 bed., newly furnished, gas CH; rent £480/cal.mth.

At Balfe Sq., Crumlin—beautiful 2-bed. town house, recently furnished, solid-fuel CH; rent £380/cal.mth.

At Ormond Pk, Templeogue—3-bed. semi., fully furnished with all amenities including oil CH; suit four sharing; rent £500/cal.mth.

At Oak Rd, Palmerstown—cosy furnished 1-bed. bungalow, no CH; rent £250/cal.mth.

At Ash Pk, Dunshaughlin—21 km from Dublin, unfurnished 4-bed. bungalow, double garage, oil CH, fitted kitchen; rent £610/cal.mth.

At Sarsfield Rd, Lucan—new 4-bed. det., unfurnished, gas CH, alarm; first letting; £550/cal.mth.

At Barton Rd, Dundrum—4-bed. det., fully furnished, no CH; near shops and schools; £570/cal.mth.

At Airport Gdns, Swords—unfurnished bungalow, 3 bed., solid-fuel CH; £370/cal.mth.

At Howth View Rd, Sutton—luxuriously appointed det. family residence, fully furnished, in pristine condition throughout; sitting-room, dining-room, study, 5 bedrooms (1 en-suite), guest bathroom, gas CH, all mod. cons., easily maintained gardens, rent £650/cal.mth.

At Golf Links Rd, Portmarnock—luxurious det. 4 bed., fully furnished, all mod. cons., solid-fuel CH, recently fitted aluminium windows, double garage, large front and rear gardens; rent £480/cal.mth.

At Marlay Wood, Rathfarnham—opposite Marlay Park, 4-bed. semi., in excellent condition, unfurnished, oil CH, garage; rent £100/week.

At Kenilworth Sq., Rathgar—delightful 3-bed. town house, gas CH, furnished, small rear garden, parking, very private, convenient to city centre; rent £500/cal.mth.

At Ashfield Park, Tallaght—3-bed. semi., quiet location, gas CH, unfurnished, garage, close to new shopping centre; rent £370/cal.mth.

At Rathowen Pk, Terenure—3-bed. town house, quiet cul-de-sac, gas CH, fully furnished, all mod. cons., large rear garden, suit retired couple; rent £470/cal.mth.

At Vernon Drive, Rathgar—charming, mature spacious home, 4 bed., det., unfurnished, no CH, double garage; rent £580/cal.mth.

At Old County Rd, Crumlin—3-bed. semi., close to Crumlin shopping centre, fully furnished, solid-fuel CH, ample parking; rent £420/cal.mth.

At River Valley, Swords—4-bed. det., fully fitted kitchen, all mod. cons, gas CH, furnished, double garage; rent £520/cal.mth.

At Conway Ave, Kilmainham—1-bed. cottage, adjacent to St James's Hospital, newly furnished, oil CH; rent £280/cal.mth.

At Park Ave, Sandymount—mature det. residence, 5 bed., large gardens, oil CH, unfurnished; rent £450/cal.mth.

Carry out the following tasks:

Print:

[1] the entire file.

Display:

[2] all the details of those houses that are semi-detached;

[3] all the details of those houses with a rent of less than £300 per calendar month;

[4] all the details of those houses with a rent of between £350 and £450 per calendar month;

[5] the area and monthly rent for all those houses with oil-fired central heating;

[6] all the details of semi-detached houses with monthly rents between £400 and £600 inclusive;

[7] the area, rent and type of central heating, in that order, for all houses with oil-fired central heating and monthly rent of less than £500;

[8] the average rent of a three-bedroom house according to the details in this file.

Edit the file—

[9] to include details of eight other houses extracted from the 'Houses to let' section of your local newspaper.

Display:

[10] all the details of those houses with more than three bedrooms, sorted in descending order of rent.

Print:

[11] the entire file sorted in alphabetical order by area.

Chapter 4

Data-base concepts

The following concepts will be discussed in this chapter:

B. Computer filing
1. Advantages of using a computer data-base
2. Disadvantages of using a computer data-base
3. Applications suited to computer data-bases
4. Storage requirements for computer data-base files
5. Magnetic disk and tape files
6. Types of computer data-base programs

A. Manual filing
1. Manual filing systems
2. Methods of classification
3. Limitations of manual filing systems
4. Security of manual filing systems

A. Manual filing

1. Manual filing systems

In order to gain an understanding of computerised filing systems we should first look at some examples of manual filing systems, many of which are still in use today.

Vertical filing
This is a very common system, in which the files are arranged vertically (upright) in v-shaped file holders, with title strips displayed on the top edges. Each file holder is suspended from two parallel rails built into the drawer, and the cabinet usually contains four to six drawers.

A typical use for this system would be in a doctor's office for holding information on patients.

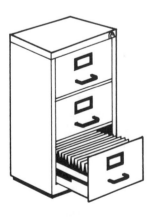

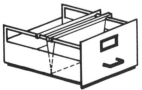

Lateral filing

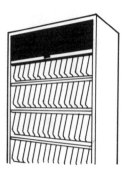

This is another common filing system, in which the files are stored side-by-side in a series of file holders rather like books in a bookshelf. The file holders are suspended within a filing cabinet, and each file has a tag that protrudes from the file holder that the user can consult.

An example of an area where this kind of filing system would be found is a college administration office, for holding information on the students.

Horizontal filing

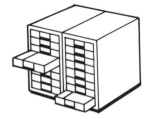 

Large diagrams, maps and plans need to be stored horizontally in drawers. Some documents must not be folded, and it is important that the drawers used are large enough to accommodate them.

This system would be used by cartographers to store large-scale Ordnance Survey maps.

Rotary filing

With this method the files are inserted into shelves on a two or three-tier rotating circular stand, usually placed near the user's desk. Documents or files can be quite easily retrieved by simply rotating the appropriate tier.

A case in which this filing system might be used is a small wholesaler's office where the secretary must frequently access and store information on different customers.

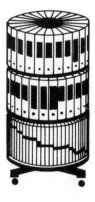

Microfilm

With a microfilm system the documents or files to be stored are photographically reduced and copied onto film. This is usually in the form of either 16 mm film strip or **microfiche**, sheets of film measuring 105 by 148 mm. A full roll of 16 mm microfilm can hold the images of about three thousand A4 pages; a microfiche usually holds ninety-eight A4 pages.

One drawback of this system is the necessity to use a viewing device to enlarge the image. Nevertheless microfilm is quite popular, especially where there is little room for filing cabinets. Microfiche is used by bookshops to store information on books in print.

A small roll of microfilm can contain information from a large stack of documents.

Card files

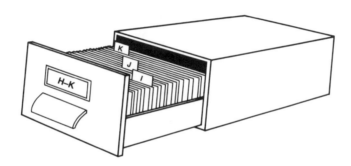

This system usually consists of a box of small cards, each one containing typewritten (or neatly handwritten) information. The cards are arranged alphabetically or in some other systematic way, and may also be secured by a rod passing through a hole in each card. Guide cards can be added at intervals to help in retrieval of information.

Card files are widely used by libraries, as the index can be used to give additional information on authors, titles, subjects, and location.

2. Methods of classification

One or more methods of classification can be used with any filing system. We will now examine some of the more common methods:

Alphabetical

Documents or files are arranged with their most useful aspect—usually the surnames of the customers to which they refer—in alphabetical order. This is the most common method of sorting files.

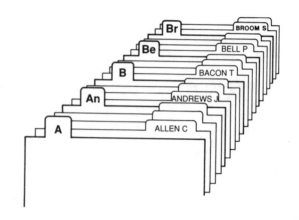

Chronological

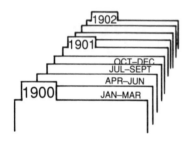

Documents or files are arranged in date order; for example, a solicitor might decide to hold her client files in the order of the dates on which she will represent each one in court.

Geographical

Documents or files are arranged according to the geographical locations of the subjects; for example, a salesman might decide to arrange his files in this way so that he could call on his customers in a particular area on the same day.

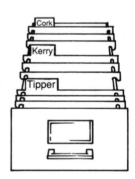

Subject

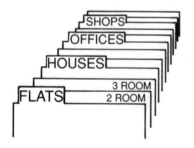

Documents or files are arranged according to subject headings; for example, an estate agent might sort the files on all the properties she is at present trying to sell according to whether they are houses, shops, offices, flats, and so on.

Numerical

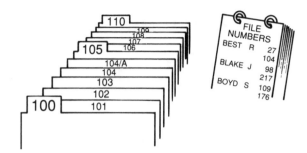

Each file is given a number, and the files are arranged numerically in ascending order. The people who need to use the files would have access to an index, which would contain the customers' names and give the corresponding file numbers. This system ensures a certain amount of confidentiality: unauthorised staff would have difficulty in getting access to information on a particular person without the index. A doctor might use this system to arrange files on patients.

Combined classifications

Files are often arranged in a manner that borrows from a number of the different methods already mentioned. Classified telephone directories are an example where information on various services is arranged primarily by subject, but within each subject classification the suppliers are arranged in alphabetical order.

3. Limitations of manual filing systems

The main limitations of manual filing systems are:

- centralisation
- difficulty in using a number of search criteria
- maintenance
- large storage requirements

Centralisation

Many filing systems are centralised. This means that all the documents and files are held together in the same place. This can give rise to a number of problems:

- A person who frequently uses the system and whose office is some distance from the place where the files are kept would lose considerable time accessing and returning files;

- A number of people cannot borrow the same file at the same time;

- An accident such as a fire or burst water pipe in the area where the files are kept could destroy a great deal of important information.

Difficulty in using a number of search criteria

Searching for information using a number of different criteria is very tedious when using a manual filing system. Repeated manual searches and sorting of the files are usually needed to retrieve the required information.

A person might have a preference for a three-bedroomed house with oil-fired central heating and an oak kitchen in the £60,000–80,000 price range. It could take an estate agent some time to extract all the properties that meet these criteria from the files in the filing cabinet.

Maintenance

The maintenance of a manual filing system is usually taken to mean keeping the files up to date.

An estate agent with hundreds of different types of property for sale in many areas would have great difficulty in keeping files up to date. Properties are continually coming on the market and others are being sold, and the information on the estate agent's files would vary considerably from week to week.

Large storage requirements

Manual filing systems can take up a large amount of floor space, and in many organisations the available space is limited. Some offices have a lot of floor space taken up by bulky filing cabinets. This can be very expensive, as office rents are in proportion to the floor area.

4. Security of manual filing systems

It is important that a filing system be made as secure as possible, for two main reasons:

- confidentiality
- accidental damage

Confidentiality

Confidentiality of files should always be maintained. Access to a filing cabinet in a doctor's office, which contains patients' case histories, must only be available to the doctor concerned.

A manual filing system can be made more secure by:

- providing only authorised staff with keys to the area where the files are kept;
- appointing one person to be responsible for maintaining a filing system;
- maintaining a log-book of the names of those people who have borrowed files.

Accidental damage

To secure a manual filing system against damage by fire, water or natural disaster is difficult. Two of the more common measures taken to safeguard manual filing systems against accidental damage are:

- storing of files in steel cabinets;
- holding an up-to-date contingency or 'back-up' filing system in another place.

B. Computer filing

The limitations of manual filing systems have contributed greatly to the growth in popularity of computers as a means of storing information. As we saw in chapter 2, a computer equipped with a data-base program not only allows us to store files but also allows us to manipulate and retrieve information from those files.

The movement towards computer data-bases has both advantages and disadvantages.

1. Advantages of using a computer data-base

Speed of access

Information that is needed can be retrieved extremely quickly. The price of a new oil filter for a particular make of car can be found out immediately by a garage attendant who has access to the garage's computer data-base.

Ease of editing

Information in a data-base file can be edited with considerable ease. If an employee informs his or her company of a change of address, this change can be included in the personnel file without any difficulty.

Efficient sorting

Computer data-base users can easily sort information. The managing director of a company can obtain from the company's data-base a print-out of the names of all the employees, in alphabetical order.

Access by different users

Some computer data-bases allow multiple-user access. This means that all the users can have access to the same files. A number of branches of the same estate agency could have access to the same information on properties that are for sale.

Confidentiality

Certain users can be denied access to files containing confidential or sensitive information, by assigning passwords to authorised users.

Easier back-up

It is much easier to keep up-to-date contingency copies of important files with a data-base program than with a manual filing system.

Report generation

Many different types of report can be generated from the same file or files by the data-base program. A manager could obtain a report on all sales in the past two months from the sales file; one of the sales staff could obtain from the same file a report on sales in a particular region.

2. Disadvantages of using a computer data-base

User incompetence

A person who has not been properly trained in the use of a particular program could incorrectly update records, generate reports based on wrong criteria, or even accidentally erase important files.

System failure

A power failure could result in some files being lost. A 'head crash' on a disk could result in a disk containing important files being made unusable. (That is why it is essential that we keep up-to-date copies of important work.)

'Technophobia'

This is the fear that many people have of technology. Some people may prefer to operate outdated manual filing systems rather than have to use a microcomputer.

Non-portability

Files set up using one data-base program cannot at present be updated, searched or sorted using a different data-base program.

3. Applications suited to computer data-bases

Most applications where files are regularly updated, searched and sorted would be suited to a computer data-base. Some examples are:

Student records
Schools and colleges can use data-bases to hold details of students and their progress.

Police records
The Garda Síochána can use computer data-bases to hold records of people who have broken the law.

Company sales files
In a company that maintains sales records on a computer data-base, the file can be updated at a certain time each week by entering all the transactions for that week. This technique of updating a file at one time with all the transactions that have occurred in a given period is known as **batch processing.**

Airline reservations
Computer data-bases are used by airlines to hold information on departure dates and times and on the availability of seats on various flights. When a travel agent books a seat on a flight, the transaction is used by the computer to immediately update a particular file; this technique is known as **real-time processing.**

Teletext
Television stations provide information to the public through their teletext services, such as the Aertel service operated by RTE. These are large data-bases containing information ranging from flight arrival times to the latest sports results. Teletext allows you to view the information in the data-base but not to alter it in any way.

4. Storage requirements for computer data-base files

The amount of computer storage or 'memory' required to hold a file will depend on whether the file comprises fixed-length or variable-length records.

A **fixed-length record** is one that contains a predetermined number of fields and in which each field has a maximum width.

A **variable-length record** is one that does not contain a predetermined number of fields and in which the individual fields may vary in length from one record to the next.

Many data-base programs allow only fixed-length records. As we saw in chapter 2, we must define the number of fields in each record and the width of each field.

Examine the following fixed-length records:

NAME	AGE	PHONE_NO
MAC LOCHLAINN P	9	(051) 45689
HARRINGTON R	9	(01) 7848859
MURPHY S	11	(041) 39344

The field widths must be defined to accommodate the longest item of data in each field, as follows:

Field name	Field width	
NAME	15	—to accommodate MAC LOCHLAINN P
AGE	2	—to accommodate 11
PHONE_NO	12	—to accommodate (01) 7848859

We can now say that:

Record length = the sum of the field widths

At this level we are not interested in the storage requirements of field and record markers, which serve to tell the computer where the beginning and end of fields and records are.

The combined length of the three records in our example above is 87, and yet there are only 73 characters that make up the data items in the three records outlined above. This is wasteful of computer memory and the disk storage space available.

A data-base program that allows variable-length records will be more economical with memory and disk space than one that only allows fixed-length records. The main disadvantage of variable-length records is that, because the record lengths are different, they require extra processing.

Calculating file size

As we saw in chapter 1, a byte is the amount of storage space required for one character. We can easily calculate the number of bytes needed to store a file containing fixed-length or variable-length records.

Fixed-length records:

File size = record length × number of records

Variable-length records:

File size = sum of all record lengths

Example 1

Let us assume that a file consists of 100 records and that the storage space required for each record is 124 bytes. The amount of storage space required to hold the file is therefore 12,400 bytes or approximately 12.1 kilobytes (1 kb = 1,024 bytes).

Many data-base programs, because of memory restrictions, have an upper limit on the length of fields. They also have an upper limit on the number of fields in each record, and an upper limit on the number of records in a single file. You should check the maximum file, record and field lengths allowed by your data-base program.

We can calculate the number of records that we can store on a magnetic disk or tape, provided the storage requirement of each record and the capacity of the disk or tape are known.

Example 2

Let us say that the storage requirement of each record is 350 bytes and the disk capacity is 360 kb. We use the following formula in our calculation:

$$\text{Number of records} = \frac{\text{Disk capacity (kb)} \times 1,024}{\text{Storage requirement of one record}}$$

The maximum number of records that can be accommodated is therefore 1,053.

5. Magnetic disk and tape files

As we have seen, magnetic disks and tapes are used to store files outside the computer. We must now examine the various ways in which files can be organised on magnetic storage media: as serial files, sequential files, or random files.

Serial files

When records in a file are copied from the computer's memory to disk or tape in any order, then the file is known as a serial file.

Sequential files

When the records in a file are copied to disk or tape sorted in order of the key field or fields, then the file is known as a sequential file.

Employee records may be stored sequentially on disk or tape using the employee number as the key field. Each week the records could be retrieved in sequence and each employee's wages calculated by the computer.

Random files

This file organisation only applies to files stored on disk. The records are placed on the disk apparently at random: there is no obvious relationship between their positions.

A mathematical formula is derived which when applied to the key field of any record generates a number: the location (disk address) of the record on the disk. The read-write head of the disk drive moves directly to where the record is stored or where it is about to be stored. The record is then retrieved from or placed in this position.

6. Types of computer data-base programs

In our data-base assignments in chapter 3 we only concerned ourselves with the simplest type of data-base, called a **flat-file data-base**. This is one in which each record in a file must have the same structure, and records in one file are not related to records in another file.

We will now briefly examine two types of data-base program that offer the user more powerful facilities to manipulate data stored on computer. These are relational data-bases and programmable data-bases.

Relational data-bases

These are the most common data-base programs available. They have the ability to link two or more files through at least one common field; the user will then be offered a wider choice of search criteria for the selection of data.

Relational data-base programs also allow a number of files that are linked to be updated by the user through one operation. For example, assuming that a customer file and product file are linked by a common field, for example the product code field, the user could update both files simultaneously with an invoice.

Programmable data-bases

Some data-base programs are equipped with their own data-base programming language. The user, by learning how to program in this language, can construct files and reports to suit his or her exact needs.

Most programmable data-base programs nowadays also offer a menu-driven system. Anyone who is unfamiliar with the programming language can still carry out quite advanced work using this system.

Both relational and programmable data-base programs can also be used to set up and manage a simple flat-file data-base.

Summary

In this chapter we investigated manual filing methods and classification systems. We examined how a computer equipped with a data-base program can be used to store information, and saw the ease with which information can be edited, retrieved, and sorted.

With the development of microcomputers with faster processing speeds and greater disk storage capacities, we can expect that the trend away from traditional manual filing systems and towards computer data-bases will continue.

Questions

Multi-choice questions

1. Which classification system describes the order of items in the following list: (*a*) alphabetical, (*b*) numerical, (*c*) subject, or (*d*) chronological?

Chicken chasseur £4.50
Lasagne £4.75
Smoked cod £5.50
Sirloin steak £7.30

2. The list below gives the field names and field lengths of all the fields in the structure of a fixed-length record. How many bytes would be required to store 500 of these records: (*a*) 50, (*b*) 500, (*c*) 2,500, or (*d*) 25,000?

Field name	Length
Company	22
Area	15
Product	10
Employees	3

3. Which of the following files is most likely to consist of records containing large amounts of textual data?

(*a*) personnel file
(*b*) stock file
(*c*) milk delivery file
(*d*) price catalogue file

4. The character C3PO was a big star in the film *Star Wars*. Would you classify his name as:

(*a*) alphabetic
(*b*) alphanumeric
(*c*) scientific
(*d*) imaginary?

5. Which of the following statements is false? A file—

    (a) is a collection of similar records
    (b) can consist of fixed-length or variable-length records
    (c) can consist of fixed-length and variable-length records
    (d) can sometimes consist of fixed-length records

6. A diskette has 350 kb available for the storage of data. How many fixed-length records can be accommodated if each record can contain 512 characters?

    (a) 70
    (b) 700
    (c) 1,024
    (d) 3,584

7. When a record in a file is updated as soon as a transaction occurs, is this called:

    (a) real-time processing
    (b) batch processing
    (c) direct-action processing
    (d) fast-line processing?

8. Which of the following statements is true? Bar-code readers—

    (a) are only used in supermarkets
    (b) can be used both as input and output devices
    (c) are useful when data must be entered quickly into a computer system
    (d) require that the user be competent in keyboarding

9. In sorting a file, which of the following is most efficient in its use of disk space?

    (a) sorting
    (b) multi-level sorting
    (c) indexing
    (d) min-level indexing?

10. Which of the following statements is false? Altering a particular record's structure could mean—

    (a) adding new data to some of the fields
    (b) lengthening one or more fields
    (c) adding a new field
    (d) deleting a very long field

Short-answer questions

1. Give examples of applications that would use the following filing classifications:

    (a) alphabetical
    (b) subject
    (c) chronological
    (d) numerical

Why would this be the best classification for each application you have chosen?

2. Give the limitations of a centralised manual filing system.

3. Give three methods you would use to ensure the integrity of data stored in a manual filing system.

4. Illustrate, by means of an example, the use of an index in a manual filing system.

5. Give, with reasons, two examples of operations that would require the use of a computer data-base program to store and manage files.

6. Give, with reasons, two examples of operations that would not require a computer data-base program to store and manage files.

7. Explain why it is necessary to define field lengths, field names and field types when defining the record structure of a file on computer.

8. Distinguish between flat-file and relational data-bases. Describe one operation where it would be necessary to use a relational data-base program to store and manage files.

9. What is a programmable data-base management system? What advantages, if any, would it have for the user over a flat-file data-base program?

10. Suggest what the term 'user-friendliness' might mean with respect to computer data-base programs, and explain how one data-base program might be more 'user-friendly' than another.

Glossary of data-base terms

batch processing: the technique of updating a file at one time with all the transactions that have occurred in a given period.

data-base: a collection of related information about a subject, organised in a way that provides the means for retrieving and sorting the information, drawing conclusions, and making decisions.

data-base management system (DBMS): a computer program used for creating data-bases and that provides the tools for inserting, retrieving, modifying and deleting information and for producing relevant reports from the data-base.

data entry form: a form layout on the screen that facilitates the entering of information into a data-base file. Only one record is displayed at a time, and the fields within each record are usually listed vertically.

field: a space for a specified piece of information in a record.

file: a collection of similar records.

fixed-length field: a field that is capable of holding a predetermined maximum number of characters.

fixed-length record: a record that is capable of holding a predetermined number of fixed-length records.

flat-file data-base: a data-base in which all the files are treated individually by the program and are not linked in any way.

flat-file data-base program: a program that stores, organises and retrieves information from one file at a time.

index: a small file containing 'pointers' or information about the physical location of records in a data-base file. When searching or sorting, the data-base program uses the index rather than the full data-base.

microfiche: a form of microfilm in which documents are photographically reduced and copied onto small sheets of film.

microfilm: an information storage system in which documents are photographically reduced and copied onto 16 mm film strip.

multi-level sort: a sort that uses two fields, a primary sort field and a secondary sort field, to determine the order in which records are arranged.

multi-user system: a system that allows more than one person to have access to the data-base program and files at the same time.

programmable data-base: a data-base system that has its own programming language, allowing the user to structure files and reports according to specific needs.

random access: a method that allows the system to retrieve information by going directly to a specific part of a disk rather than having to go through all the preceding tracks and sectors.

real-time processing: the technique of updating a file when the operator is 'on-line' to the CPU and the updating is carried out immediately by the computer.

relational data-base: a data-base system that can link two or more files together through at least one common field. Such a program allows the user to update two or more linked files simultaneously in the same operation.

sequential file: a file in which the records are arranged in a particular order, usually ascending or descending order of key field.

serial file: a method in which the records in a file are not physically arranged in any particular order on a disk or tape.

sort: an operation that arranges data in a particular order.

variable-length field: a field whose length varies according to the contents of the field at a particular time.

variable-length record: a record in which the number of fields may vary from that of other records in the same file. Variable-length records usually consist of variable-length fields.

Section C

Spreadsheets

Chapter 5

Introduction to spreadsheets

What is a spreadsheet?

A spreadsheet is a screen image of a form or matrix made up of rows and columns in which automatic and interconnected calculations are made.

In 1978 an American business student named Dan Bricklin got very tired of adding columns of numbers and then adding them again and again when only a few changes had been made. He approached a programming friend for help in solving his problem, and they came up with a program called Visicalc, written for the Apple II computer. There are now many other spreadsheets available, such as Excel, Lotus 1-2-3, Multiplan, Quickcalc, Supercalc, and Viewsheet. Most of these programs contain many new features.

What does a spreadsheet look like?

	A	B	C	D	E	F
1		CELL B1				
2						
3						
4						CELL F4
5						
6	CELL A6					
7						
8						
9				CELL D9		
10						
11						
12						
13						
14						
15						
16						
17						
18						
19						
20					CELL E20	

Each **column** in a spreadsheet is usually labelled with a letter, and each **row** with a number. The panel where a column and a row cross each other is a **cell**. Where column A and row 6 meet is cell A6; where column B and row 1 meet is cell B1.

A small spreadsheet might contain 200 rows and 60 columns; this means that it would have 12,000 cells. The size of a computer screen would not allow all these cells to be seen together: usually a screen can show about 6 columns and 20 rows at a time. Any movement outside or below the edge of the screen will mean losing the display of some information from the previous screen.

In fact the display can be considered as a movable window that can view only one 'page' or screen of the spreadsheet at any time.

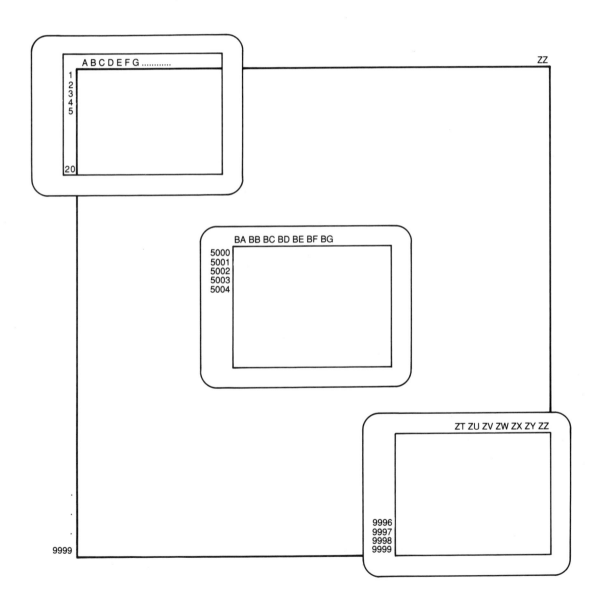

What can be put into a spreadsheet?

Any of three types of data can be entered in a cell: a value, a label, or a formula.

A **value** (or 'numeric') is any number on which calculations can be performed. This excludes dates and times, numbers followed by units of measurement, and numbers at the beginning of headings. Also, large numbers must be entered without the traditional comma (or, in modern practice, the space) used as the 'thousand marker', as this would prevent calculations being carried out on them; most spreadsheets, however, can add such markers to the results.

A **label** is any non-numeric data. Normally it is text used as headings, such as the labels INCOME, EXPENSES and PROFIT in the example below, but can also include numbers that are not used for calculation purposes, for example year headings.

A **formula** is any algebraic expression used for performing calculations on different cells. In cell C8 in the illustration below, +C5–C6 is a formula that subtracts the contents of cell C6 from the contents of cell C5. When a formula is typed into a cell, the result of the calculation is displayed in that cell, not the formula.

Remember to use the asterisk (*) as the multiplication sign, the stroke (/) for division, and the circumflex (^) for 'to the power of', and to leave no spaces between numbers and signs.

	A	B	C	D	E	F
1		PROFIT STATEMENT, 1989 TO 1990				
2						
3			1989	1990	1991	
4						
5		INCOME	10000	20000	40000	
6		EXPENSES	5000	8000	17000	
7						
8		PROFIT	+C5–C6	+D5–D6	+E5–E6	
9						
10						

Example 1

Personal budget

The following topics will be discussed using example 1 below:

1. Setting up the spreadsheet
2. Entering formulas
3. The summation function
4. Improving the appearance of the spreadsheet

5. Replication
6. Editing the spreadsheet
7. Considering 'what if?' situations
8. The 'logical if' function
9. Other facilities

Explanation
This example contains a record of personal income and weekly expenditure of a family for four weeks.

Data entry
The only items entered directly are the wages and the various expenses during the week. All other totals and figures are worked out automatically.

	A	B	C	D	E	F
		WEEK 1	WEEK 2	WEEK 3	WEEK 4	TOTAL
1	PERSONAL BUDGET	WEEK 1	WEEK 2	WEEK 3	WEEK 4	TOTAL
2						
3						
4	OPENING BALANCE	0	12.14	9.82	3.28	
5	WAGES	170	155	150	182	657
6						
7	TOTAL MONEY	170	167.14	159.82	185.28	
8						
9	EXPENSES					
10						
11	CAR EXPENSES	22.45	22	11	18.33	73.78
12	FOOD	40.86	43.77	51.67	35.45	171.75
13	BILLS	13	23	26	33	95
14	ENTERTAINMENT	18	10	5.32	29.55	62.87
15	BANK SAVINGS	8	8	8	8	32
16	MORTGAGE	50.55	50.55	50.55	50.55	202.2
17	MISC.	5	0	4	10	19
18						
19						
20	TOTAL EXPENSES	157.86	157.32	156.54	184.88	656.6
21	CLOSING BAL.	12.14	9.82	3.28	0.4	
22						
23						
24						
25						

1. Setting up the spreadsheet

In the example above, column A contains labels that explain the contents of rows 4 to 21. The labels WEEK 1 etc. are column headings that identify which week the figures in the columns relate to.

The width of column A will have to be changed to accommodate the labels in it. This is done by giving the appropriate command. Here the width is changed from the default setting of 9 characters to 18 characters wide. On most spreadsheets it is possible to change all or just one column width.

The labels in the example would be typed into the blank sheet first. Formulas will be used to calculate totals and closing and opening balances. The information on income and expenses would be then typed in each week.

The opening balance in week 1 is any spare money we have. For the other weeks it is the difference between the total we receive in a week and the total expenses, i.e. the previous week's closing balance.

2. Entering formulas

The TOTAL MONEY is the opening balance plus net wages (wages after tax). The formula in B7 would therefore be +B4+B5. (Remember that when a formula is entered in a cell it is the result that is displayed, not the formula.)

To total the expenses we must again use a formula in B20. This would be +B11+B12+B13+ B14+B15+B16+B17.

The CLOSING BAL. is the difference between total income and total expenses this week. The formula to be typed in B21 therefore is +B7−B20.

The opening balance for week 2 will be the closing balance for week 1. So in C4 we enter the formula +B21.

For the next three weeks the formulas will be repeated, except for cell references. The formulas for week 2 are:

```
Cell C4: + B21
Cell C7: + C4 + C5
Cell C20: + C11+ C12 + C13 + C14 + C15 + C16 + C17
Cell C21: + C7 − C20
```

Similarly the formulas for week 3 will be:

```
Cell D4: + C21
Cell D7: + D4 + D5
Cell D20: + D11 + D12 + D13 + D14 + D15 + D16 + D17
Cell D21: . . .
```

Try working out the formulas for week 4 yourself.

```
Cell E4: . . .
Cell E7: . . .
Cell E20: . . .
Cell E21: . . .
```

Finally, the totals for the month are entered. The formula for total wages is B5+C5+D5+E5. This will be entered in cell F5. Similarly the formula for total car expenses will be +B11+C11+D11+E11. This would be entered in cell F11. Try working out the formulas for the following cells:

Cell F12: . . .
Cell F13: . . .
Cell F14: . . .
Cell F15: . . .
Cell F16: . . .
Cell F17: . . .
Cell F20: . . .

3. The summation function

You may have noticed that the formulas in cells B20, C20, D20 and E20 are very long. They would be even longer if we had any more expenses.

We can use the summation or total function to add up whole columns or rows of numbers. Instead of typing all the parts of the formula we only have to type in the first and last cell references. In BBC Quickcalc the formula in cell B20 would be SUM(B11,B17); in Lotus 1-2-3 it would be @SUM(B11..B17). Similarly the formula in F5 (+B5+C5+D5+E5) would be replaced with SUM(B5,E5) or @SUM(B5..E5). Check your own spreadsheet program for the formula for this function.

Write down on a page all the shorter summation formulas required to add up the rows and columns in this example.

Other mathematical functions are available on most spreadsheets, for example the 'average' function, which will find the mean of a range of numbers. Other mathematical functions include sin, cos, tan, etc. More advanced financial and statistical functions are available on some spread-sheets.

4. Improving the appearance of the spreadsheet

Changing the format of numbers

You will notice that the money amounts in our example are very untidy in appearance. This is because all the numbers have not got the same number of decimal places. For money amounts of course this is usually two. If possible also the pound sign should be displayed in front of the amounts. A special command can be given to change the required range or group of numbers to this style, called 'cash format'. (Other formats are possible and are discussed in chapter 7.)

Aligning the labels

You will notice also that the week labels are not exactly in line with the amounts below them. This is because numbers are automatically displayed **flush right** or aligned on the right (i.e. the last digit is in the extreme right of the cell), whereas text is automatically displayed **flush left** or aligned on the left (i.e. the first character of the label is in the extreme left of the cell). However, it is possible to change the alignment of any cell to flush right, flush left, or centred.

Here we will give the command to change the week labels to flush right and change the money amounts to cash format. Our spreadsheet should now look like this:

	A	B	C	D	E	F
1	PERSONAL BUDGET	WEEK 1	WEEK 2	WEEK 3	WEEK 4	TOTAL
2						
3						
4	OPENING BALANCE	£0.00	£12.14	£9.82	£3.28	
5	WAGES	£170.00	£155.00	£150.00	£182.00	£657.00
6						
7	TOTAL MONEY	£170.00	£167.14	£159.82	£185.28	
8						
9	EXPENSES					
10						
11	CAR EXPENSES	£22.45	£22.00	£11.00	£18.33	£73.78
12	FOOD	£40.86	£43.77	£51.67	£35.45	£171.75
13	BILLS	£13.00	£23.00	£26.00	£33 .00	£95.00
14	ENTERTAINMENT	£18.00	£10.00	£5.32	£29.55	£62.87
15	BANK SAVINGS	£8.00	£8.00	£8.00	£8.00	£32.00
16	MORTGAGE	£50.55	£50.55	£50.00	£50.55	£202.20
17	MISC.	£5.00	£0.00	£4.00	£10.00	£19.00
18						
19						
20	TOTAL EXPENSES	£157.86	£157.32	£156.54	£184.88	£656.60
21	CLOSING BAL.	£12.14	£9.82	£3.28	£0.40	
22						
23						

5. Replication

You will have noticed when entering the data in our example that there is a lot of repetitive typing of formulas. If you had to expand the model to accommodate fifty-two weeks you would be very tired after typing in all the formulas! However, all spreadsheets allow you to 'replicate' or copy formulas or text from one area of the spreadsheet to another.

There are three levels of copying or replicating to begin with: straight copying, range copying, and formula copying.

Straight copying

This is where one item (whether a number or label) is copied from one cell to another, and can be used when you want to avoid retyping names or headings. It is done by entering the appropriate command and the identification of the cells you want to *copy from* ('source cell') and *copy to* ('target cell').

Range copying
This involves entering the 'source range' of cells to be copied and the 'target range' of cells to be copied to.

Formula copying
There are three types of formula copying: **absolute**, where there is no change in the cell references when copied; **relative**, where the copied formulas change cell references according to their position; and **absolute and relative**, where some cell references in the formula do not change when copied and others do. For example, copying down a column:

Absolute	Relative	Absolute-relative	Relative-absolute
A1*B1	A1*B1	A1*B1	A1*B1
A1*B1	A2*B2	A1*B2	A2*B1
A1*B1	A3*B3	A1*B3	A3*B1
A1*B1	A4*B4	A1*B4	A4*B1
A1*B1	A5*B5	A1*B5	A5*B1

(The formula to be copied is the first one in each column. Notice that only the row numbers change by one when copying relative cell references down a column.)

Copying across rows:

Absolute	A1*B1	A1*B1	A1*B1	A1*B1
Relative	A1*B1	B1*C1	C1*D1	D1*E1
Absolute-relative	A1*B1	A1*C1	A1*D1	A1*E1
Relative-absolute	A1*B1	B1*B1	C1*B1	D1*B1

(The formula to be copied is the first one in each row. Notice that only the column letter changes by one when copying relative cell references across a row.)

In the personal budget example above we could have copied most of our formulas. We could have typed the formula +B4+B5 in B7, then copied it across to C7, D7 and E7 using relative cell references, so that each cell reference would change across the row. This would be done by identifying B7 as the cell to copy from and the range C7 to E7 as the range to copy to.

If we were to copy B7 using absolute cell references or a combination of absolute and relative cell references we would get incorrect totals. This would be the result from the different alternatives:

Copy	from B7	to C7	to D8	to E7
Absolute	+B4+B5	+B4+B5	+B4+B5	+B4+B5
Relative	+B4+B5	+C4+C5	+D4+D5	+E4+E5
Absolute-relative	+B4+B5	+B4+C5	+B4+D5	+B4+E5
Relative-absolute	+B4+B5	+C4+B5	+D4+B5	+E4+B5

Results	B7	C7	D8	E7
Absolute	170	170	170	170
Relative	170	167.14	159.82	185.28
Absolute-relative	170	155	150	182
Relative-absolute	170	182.14	179.82	173.28

Replication could also be used for the formulas in rows 20 and 21. For row 20 we would copy the formula from cell B20 to the cells in the range C20 to F20, using relative cell references. In the same way we would copy the formula in cell B21 (+B7–B20) to the cells in the range C21 to E21.

Copying with relative cell references could also be used for the formulas in column F, from cell F11 to the cells in the range F12 to F16.

The importance of replication

It is the replication function that gives the computer spreadsheet its real power. Once the core or original formulas have been entered it is only a matter of replicating them as far as the memory of your computer will allow. Spreadsheets can be constructed very quickly and easily using replication, which is their main advantage over manual systems. In our example we could expand the model to cover fifty-two weeks by simple replication of the formulas: no new formulas would need to be typed in.

6. Editing the spreadsheet

Simple editing

If we want to change any information on the spreadsheet we simply type over it or use the editing facility to insert or delete some characters. In this example we want to change the contents of cell A5 to read NET WAGES instead of WAGES. We will use the editing facility, type the word NET and then press [enter].

Inserting rows or columns

In our example we might decide to enter a blank row in row 9 to separate the expenses more clearly from other data on the sheet. To do this we use the appropriate command for inserting a row. The result will be that the present contents of row 9 will move down one row; all other rows will also move down one row.

When we do this the computer automatically changes all formulas that are affected by the move. The formula for total expenses will change from @SUM(B11.. B16) to @SUM(B12..B17), while the formula to calculate the closing balance will change from +B7−B20 to +B7−B21. The opening balance formulas will also change, from +B21 to +B22. In fact most of the formulas in the spreadsheet will change because of the insertion of the row.

If we insert a new column, the information is moved across to the right, and again any formulas that are affected will change automatically.

Our spreadsheet will look like this after these two changes have been carried out:

	A	B	C	D	E	F
1	PERSONAL BUDGET	WEEK 1	WEEK 2	WEEK 3	WEEK 4	TOTAL
2						
3						
4	OPENING BALANCE	£0.00	£12.14	£9.82	£3.28	
5	NET WAGES	£170.00	£155.00	£150.00	£182.00	£657.00
6						
7	TOTAL MONEY	£170.00	£167.14	£159.82	£185.28	
8						
9						
10	EXPENSES					
11						
12	CAR EXPENSES	£22.45	£22.00	£11.00	£18.33	£73.78
13	FOOD	£40.86	£43.77	£51.67	£35.45	£171.75
14	BILLS	£13.00	£23.00	£26.00	£33 .00	£95.00
15	ENTERTAINMENT	£18.00	£10.00	£5.32	£29.55	£62.87
16	BANK SAVINGS	£8.00	£8.00	£8.00	£8.00	£32.00
17	MORTGAGE	£50.55	£50.55	£50.00	£50.55	£202.20
18	MISC.	£5.00	£0.00	£4.00	£10.00	£19.00
19						
20						
21	TOTAL EXPENSES	£157.86	£157.32	£156.54	£184.88	£656.60
22	CLOSING BAL.	£12.14	£9.82	£3.28	£0.40	

Perhaps we forgot to include some expenses. In that case we would need to insert a new row and heading containing the new information. Let us say the forgotten expense was pocket money of £1 a week given to one of the children, and the information is to be inserted after the food expense. When this row is inserted the formulas and amounts will change automatically to reflect this: for example the total expenses formula will now be @SUM(B12..B19). Note that in week 4 we have overspent by £3.60.

The spreadsheet will look like this after inserting the new pocket money row:

	A	B	C	D	E	F
1	PERSONAL BUDGET	WEEK 1	WEEK 2	WEEK 3	WEEK 4	TOTAL
2						
3						
4	OPENING BALANCE	£0.00	£11.14	£7.82	£0.28	
5	NET WAGES	£170.00	£155.00	£150.00	£182.00	£657.00
6						
7	TOTAL MONEY	£170.00	£166.14	£157.82	£182.28	
8						
9						
10	EXPENSES					
11						
12	CAR EXPENSES	£22.45	£22.00	£11.00	£18.33	£73.78
13	FOOD	£40.86	£43.77	£51.67	£35.45	£171.75
14	POCKET MONEY	£1.00	£1.00	£1.00	£1.00	£4.00
15	BILLS	£13.00	£23.00	£26.00	£33 .00	£95.00
16	ENTERTAINMENT	£18.00	£10.00	£5.32	£29.55	£62.87
17	BANK SAVINGS	£8.00	£8.00	£8.00	£8.00	£32.00
18	MORTGAGE	£50.55	£50.55	£50.00	£50.55	£202.20
19	MISC.	£5.00	£0.00	£4.00	£10.00	£19.00
20						
21						
22	TOTAL EXPENSES	£158.86	£158.32	£157.54	£185.88	£660.60
23	CLOSING BAL.	£11.14	£7.82	£0.82	(£3.60)	
24						
25						

7. Considering 'what if?' situations

When the spreadsheet is set up we can experiment with the data to consider the effect of different figure or policy changes. These are called 'what if?' calculations.

In the example above we could ask ourselves, what if we decided not to bring the car to work? This would mean that we would only spend £10 a week on car expenses. All we would have to do is type over the amounts in the car expenses row with the new amount, £10. All the totals will be recalculated for us. Note the saving on the weekly balances.

Any number in the spreadsheet can be changed to see what effect it might have on our total budget. On a more complex example involving many thousands of calculations, this ability to recalculate is invaluable for decision-making.

Our spreadsheet will look like this after the car expenses are changed:

	A	B	C	D	E	F
1	PERSONAL BUDGET	WEEK 1	WEEK 2	WEEK 3	WEEK 4	TOTAL
2						
3						
4	OPENING BALANCE	£0.00	£23.59	£32.27	£25.73	
5	NET WAGES	£170.00	£155.00	£150.00	£182.00	£657.00
6						
7	TOTAL MONEY	£170.00	£178.59	£182.27	£207.73	
8						
9						
10	EXPENSES					
11						
12	CAR EXPENSES	£10.00	£10.00	£10.00	£10.00	£40.00
13	FOOD	£40.86	£43.77	£51.67	£35.45	£171.75
14	POCKET MONEY	£1.00	£1.00	£1.00	£1.00	£4.00
15	BILLS	£13.00	£23.00	£26.00	£33.00	£95.00
16	ENTERTAINMENT	£18.00	£10.00	£5.32	£29.55	£62.87
17	BANK SAVINGS	£8.00	£8.00	£8.00	£8.00	£32.00
18	MORTGAGE	£50.55	£50.55	£50.55	£50.55	£202.20
19	MISC.	£5.00	£0.00	£4.00	£10.00	£19.00
20						
21						
22	TOTAL EXPENSES	£146.41	£146.32	£156.54	£177.55	£626.82
23	CLOSING BAL.	£23.59	£32.27	£25.73	£30.18	
24						

8. The 'logical if' function

Is the profit this year greater than last year? Has the aeroplane been overloaded with luggage? The answers to these questions are either true or false. These are considered logical questions, i.e. those having true or false answers.

Most spreadsheet programs allow you to employ a formula to ask a question and generate a true or false response. The general pattern this formula takes is:

If (*condition, true response, false response*)

This function is very similar to the IF—THEN—ELSE command in the programming language Basic.

In the example above we could get the computer to make a decision for us. We decide to save money based on the previous week's closing balance. We have decided that if the amount left over in the previous week is greater than £10, we will save £6 in the next week; otherwise we will not save anything in the coming week.

The first week's savings will be entered by the user, and all other weeks' savings will be calculated automatically by using the 'if' function. The formula in cell C17 will be as follows:

@IF(B23>10,6,0)

This means that if the content of cell B23 (the closing balance) is greater than £10, £6 will be entered in cell C17; otherwise £0 is entered in cell C17. This formula can then be copied across the row as far as cell E17, using relative cell references.

When the formula is copied the numbers in row 17 will change to reflect this new decision, and other totals that are affected will also change. The spreadsheet will now look like this:

	A	B	C	D	E	F
1	PERSONAL BUDGET	WEEK 1	WEEK 2	WEEK 3	WEEK 4	TOTAL
2						
3						
4	OPENING BALANCE	£0.00	£23.59	£34.27	£29.73	
5	NET WAGES	£170.00	£155.00	£150.00	£182.00	£657.00
6						
7	TOTAL MONEY	£170.00	£178.59	£184.27	£211.73	
8						
9						
10	EXPENSES					
11						
12	CAR EXPENSES	£10.00	£10.00	£10.00	£10.00	£40.00
13	FOOD	£40.86	£43.77	£51.67	£35.45	£171.75
14	POCKET MONEY	£1.00	£1.00	£1.00	£1.00	£4.00
15	BILLS	£13.00	£23.00	£26.00	£33.00	£95.00
16	ENTERTAINMENT	£18.00	£10.00	£5.32	£29.55	£62.87
17	BANK SAVINGS	£8.00	£6.00	£6.00	£6.00	£26.00
18	MORTGAGE	£50.55	£50.55	£50.55	£50.55	£202.20
19	MISC.	£5.00	£0.00	£4.00	£10.00	£19.00
20						
21						
22	TOTAL EXPENSES	£146.41	£144.32	£154.54	£175.55	£620.82
23	CLOSING BAL.	£23.59	£34.27	£29.73	£36.18	
24						

'What if?' again

We could then ask the question, what would the situation be if we used the car again for work, but this time making use of the new saving policy? We would only have to change all car expense amounts back to the original figures: all the other calculations will be done for us, including the amount we would save each week. (Note that we will save nothing on the third week.)

	A	B	C	D	E	F
		WEEK 1	WEEK 2	WEEK 3	WEEK 4	TOTAL
1	PERSONAL BUDGET	WEEK 1	WEEK 2	WEEK 3	WEEK 4	TOTAL
2						
3						
4	OPENING BALANCE	£0.00	£11.14	£9.82	£10.28	
5	NET WAGES	£170.00	£155.00	£150.00	£182.00	£657.00
6						
7	TOTAL MONEY	£170.00	£166.14	£159.82	£192.28	
8						
9						
10	EXPENSES					
11						
12	CAR EXPENSES	£22.45	£22.00	£11.00	£18.33	£73.78
13	FOOD	£40.86	£43.77	£51.67	£35.45	£171.75
14	POCKET MONEY	£1.00	£1.00	£1.00	£1.00	£4.00
15	BILLS	£13.00	£23.00	£26.00	£33 .00	£95.00
16	ENTERTAINMENT	£18.00	£10.00	£5.32	£29.55	£62.87
17	BANK SAVINGS	£8.00	£6.00	£0.00	£6.00	£20.00
18	MORTGAGE	£50.55	£50.55	£50.55	£50.55	£202.20
19	MISC.	£5.00	£0.00	£4.00	£10.00	£19.00
20						
21						
22	TOTAL EXPENSES	£158.86	£156.32	£149.54	£183.88	£648.60
23	CLOSING BAL.	£11.14	£9.82	£10.28	£8.40	
24						

9. Other facilities

Most spreadsheet programs have several other useful features, which we can use to make this application work more effectively.

Quick cursor movement

It is possible on most spreadsheets to move directly to another cell. This is done by giving a command or using a function key. The name of the desired cell is requested, and the cursor moves directly to that cell. This facility is very useful when using a very large spreadsheet.

Non-scrolling titles

Selected rows and columns can be fixed on the screen so that they do not scroll off when we move to another part of the spreadsheet. If we had the budget information for fifty-two weeks in our sample spreadsheet we might need to fix column A so that the labels for each expense would be on display permanently as we go from column to column.

Printing part or all of the spreadsheet

Large spreadsheets can be printed on several sheets and the parts joined together. Selected parts of the spreadsheet can also be printed.

Only column A and F in the example above might be required on paper, so that the total amount for each expense could be noted separately. This would require copying column A into column G and marking column F and G to be printed. This would be displayed as follows:

Totals	Personal Budget
	Opening Balance
£657.00	Net Wages
	Total Money
	Expenses
£73.78	Car Expenses
£171.75	Food
£4.00	Pocket Money
£95.00	Bills
£62.87	Entertainment
£20.00	Bank Savings
£202.20	Mortgage
£19.00	Misc.
£648.60	Total Expenses
	Closing Bal..

Turning off automatic recalculation

When a new number is typed into a spreadsheet the computer automatically recalculates all other cells affected by this change. But recalculation can take a considerable time on small computers. It is possible to turn off automatic recalculation until all changes have been made; then a command can be entered to recalculate.

Using the 'look-up' function

A range of cells that have codes and corresponding values in them can be searched with the 'look-up' function. This will return a value that relates to the code requested. This function is often used to produce invoices, where product codes are entered and the price per unit is 'looked up' by the computer.

Summary of the standard facilities of a spreadsheet program

- The cursor can be moved quickly to anywhere in the spreadsheet
- Rows and columns can be inserted in existing spreadsheets
- Rows, columns and ranges of data can be deleted
- Cell display can be changed to show different formats
- Single items or ranges of data can be copied
- Formulas can be copied or replicated
- Mathematical functions are available, for example sum, average, sin, cos, tan (on some spreadsheets other functions are available, such as financial and statistical functions)
- Editing facilities are available, while information is being typed in and afterwards
- Column widths can be changed
- Data can be stored for later retrieval
- Part or all of the spreadsheet can be printed
- Logical decisions can be make on data using the 'if' function
- Coded data can be looked up using the 'look-up' function
- Non-scrolling rows and columns can be fixed on the screen when more than one screen of data is used
- Data in the spreadsheet can be protected to prevent further changes
- Some spreadsheets allow integration or links with other types of program, such as graphics and word-processor programs

Creating a spreadsheet

Before typing in a spreadsheet you should plan what you want to do. This will involve some of the following decisions:

1. What title will I give the spreadsheet?
2. What headings will I use for the rows and columns? These should be concise but descriptive.
3. Will I need to increase or decrease the width of a column, and by how much?
4. Which of the items will be a label and which a value?
5. Where will I use a formula, and can I use an built-in function?
6. Can I replicate this formula? If so, will it be relative, absolute, or a combination?
7. Should the data be displayed in a special format, for example cash format, and where?
8. What file name will I use for the spreadsheet? This name will have to be concise but should remind you of the contents of the spreadsheet when retrieving it later.

Example 2

A more complex spreadsheet

Explanation

A small airline operates a twelve-seater aeroplane between Dublin and Knock. It wants to store passenger information on a spreadsheet. The following conditions apply:

1. The basic price of a ticket is £50.
2. There is VAT at 21 per cent on the basic price of all tickets (excluding discount).
3. There is a 10 per cent discount on the basic price of all tickets for children under 12.
4. A passenger is charged an extra £1 for every 1 kg over the 20 kg luggage allowance. No VAT is charged on this extra charge.

Data entry

The only items to be typed in are the passenger information and the standard data such as ticket price, penalty charge, etc. All other figures are to be automatically calculated by the spreadsheet through the use of formulas.

Questions

1. Set up a spreadsheet for a particular flight, including the following passenger information:

Seat no.	Name	Age	Luggage (kg)
1	Brendan Bradley	45	17
2	Ciarán Collins	5	7
3	Denis Collins	11	9
4	Martin Collins	26	23
5	Aisling Doyle	42	18
6	Kevin Geraghty	7	14
7	Paul Hillery	35	21
8	Brian Laffey	17	16
9	Seán Byrne	27	10
10	Bernadette Ryan	10	20
11	Sheila Ryan	24	17
12	Deirdre White	33	4

2. Use appropriate formulas and replication to show for each passenger the ticket price, discount, VAT, and baggage penalty. Use suitable headings.

3. Save the spreadsheet as AIR.

4. Produce a print-out of the entire spreadsheet.

Solution

Decide on the following before typing in data:

1. The title: KNOCK AIRLINES. This will be put into cell A1 and B1.

2. The following row headings will be used for the standard data in cells A2 to A5. Column A must be 11 characters wide. The figures will be put opposite this information in cells B2 to B5.

PRICE	50
VAT	.21
DISCOUNT	.10
PENALTY	1

3. Column headings will be needed for the following: SEAT NO., NAME [15 characters wide], AGE, PRICE, DISCOUNT, PRICE LESS DISCOUNT, VAT, PENALTY, and TOTAL PRICE.

The spreadsheet should now look like this:

	A	B	C	D	E	F	G	H	I	J
1	KNOCK AIRLINES									
2	PRICE	50								
3	VAT	0.21								
4	DISCOUNT	0.1								
5	PENALTY	1								
6										
7										
8	SEAT NO.	NAME	AGE	LUGGAGE	PRICE	DISCOUNT	PRICE-DIS.	VAT	PENALTY	TOTAL PRICE
9										
10	1	B BRADLEY	45	17						
11	2	C COLLINS	5	7						
12	3	D COLLINS	11	9						
13	4	M COLLINS	26	23						
14	5	A DOYLE	42	18						
15	6	K GERAGHTY	7	14						
16	7	P HILLERY	35	21						
17	8	B LAFFEY	17	16						
18	9	S BYRNE	27	10						
19	10	B RYAN	10	20						
20	11	S RYAN	24	17						
21	12	D WHITE	33	4						

4. Align all headings flush right.

5. All money amounts should be changed to cash format.

6. Decide on formulas. These will be:

E10: +B2. This must be copied down the column, using an absolute cell reference, as everybody has the same basic ticket price before other considerations are taken into account.

F10: @IF(C10<12,E10*B4,0). All parts of this formula will be copied, using relative cell references, except B4, which should remain absolute down the column.

G10: +E10–F10. This will be copied down the column, using relative cell references. The formula simply subtracts the discount (if any) from the price.

H10: +G10*B3. G10 will be relative and B3 will be absolute when copied, as the VAT rate remains 21 per cent for all tickets.

I10: @IF(D10>20,(D10–20)*B5,0). All will have relative cell references, except B5 (the penalty amount, £1), which should be absolute. (D10–20) calculates the number of kilograms over the 20 kg limit.

J10: +G10+H10+I10. This gives the total price, and should be copied using relative cell references. It includes the discounted price plus the VAT and penalty charge (if any).

The final spreadsheet should look like this after the editing and copying discussed above:

	A	B	C	D	E	F	G	H	I	J
1	KNOCK AIRLINES									
2	PRICE	£50.00								
3	VAT	0.21								
4	DISCOUNT	0.1								
5	PENALTY	£1.00								
6										
7										
8	SEAT NO.	NAME	AGE	LUGGAGE	PRICE	DISCOUNT	PRICE-DIS.	VAT	PENALTY	TOTAL PRICE
9										
10	1	B BRADLEY	45	17	£50.00	£0.00	£50.00	£10.50	£0.00	£60.50
11	2	C COLLINS	5	7	£50.00	£5.00	£45.00	£9.45	£0.00	£54.45
12	3	D COLLINS	11	9	£50.00	£5.00	£45.00	£9.45	£0.00	£54.45
13	4	M COLLINS	26	23	£50.00	£0.00	£50.00	£10.50	£3.00	£63.50
14	5	A DOYLE	42	18	£50.00	£0.00	£50.00	£10.50	£0.00	£60.50
15	6	K GERAGHTY	7	14	£50.00	£5.00	£45.00	£9.45	£0.00	£54.45
16	7	P HILLERY	35	21	£50.00	£0.00	£50.00	£10.50	£1.00	£61.50
17	8	B LAFFEY	17	16	£50.00	£0.00	£50.00	£10.50	£0.00	£60.50
18	9	S BYRNE	27	10	£50.00	£0.00	£50.00	£10.50	£0.00	£60.50
19	10	B RYAN	10	20	£50.00	£5.00	£45.00	£9.45	£0.00	£54.45
20	11	S RYAN	24	17	£50.00	£0.00	£50.00	£10.50	£0.00	£60.50
21	12	D WHITE	33	4	£50.00	£0.00	£50.00	£10.50	£0.00	£60.50
22										
23										

This spreadsheet could be used again and again by the airline. The person operating the spreadsheet would enter the standard information, including name, age, and weight of luggage, and all other figures would be calculated automatically.

Also, the formulas would not need to be changed when ticket prices and other variables changed. For example, if the rate of VAT were to change, the operator would only have to change the actual rate in cell B4: no formulas would need to be altered.

Conclusion

Spreadsheets are extremely powerful and useful analytical tools. They are used by people in many different occupations, including accountants, statisticians, engineers, and scientists. They are easy to use, and complex spreadsheets can be constructed quickly by using replication and the many built-in functions and facilities we have discussed.

In the next chapter you will have an opportunity to practise using spreadsheets by working through the different assignments.

Chapter 6

Practical spreadsheet assignments

These assignments are graded, and we advise that you work through them in the order in which they are given.

Functions and commands required

As you progress through these assignments you will need to check on the functions and commands specific to your spreadsheet program. You will also be practising commands and functions learned in earlier assignments. (*Note:* If you have not got access to a printer you can display the result of that task instead.)

The functions and commands required for each assignment are as follows:

ASSIGNMENT 1
- Entering data in a spreadsheet, including labels and values
- Changing the column width
- Changing and editing the contents of a cell
- Deleting the contents of a cell
- Saving a spreadsheet
- Exiting the system

ASSIGNMENT 2
- Recalling a spreadsheet
- Inserting a column of data
- Aligning headings
- Formatting a block of cells to show one decimal place
- Inserting a row of data
- Saving and exiting

ASSIGNMENT 3
- Recalling a spreadsheet
- Adding a new column of data
- The summation function
- Finding the average of a row
- Summing a column
- Saving and exiting

ASSIGNMENT 4
Consolidation assignment

ASSIGNMENT 5
- Choosing 'cash format'
- Entering a new column of data
- Deleting a row of data
- Block copy
- Printing part of the spreadsheet

ASSIGNMENT 6
- Entering data
- Entering, adding and subtracting formulas
- Recalculating
- Save, recall, save
- Printing the spreadsheet

ASSIGNMENT 7
- Entering data
- Using a formula to multiply and add
- Summing a row
- Relative replication down a column
- Save, edit, recalculate, save
- Printing the spreadsheet

ASSIGNMENT 8
- Entering data
- Decreasing column width
- Using a formula to multiply
- Summing columns
- Using a formula to work out a percentage
- Relative replication down columns
- Relative replication across a row
- Save, edit, recalculate, save
- Printing part of the spreadsheet

ASSIGNMENT 9
- Entering data
- Using the 'maximum' and 'minimum' functions
- Using the 'average' formula
- Relative replication across rows
- Graphing data on paper
- Non-scrolling headings

ASSIGNMENT 10
- Using formulas to get a percentage
- Using formulas to add one number to a previous number
- Absolute replication down a column
- Relative replication down a column
- Using a combination of absolute and relative replication down a column
- Performing 'what if?' calculations
- Printing the spreadsheet

ASSIGNMENT 11
- Adding new data
- Entering a complex formula in a cell

ASSIGNMENT 12
- Inserting and deleting rows of data

ASSIGNMENT 13
- Creating a spreadsheet
- Using the 'look-up' function (if available)
- Use of the 'logical if' function
- Printing the spreadsheet
- Relative, absolute and combination replication

ASSIGNMENT 14
- Use of the 'look-up' function for two sets of data (if available)
- Inserting a new column

ASSIGNMENT 15
- Creating a spreadsheet
- Copying a column of data to another column
- Using the 'integer' function
- Relative replication
- Printing the spreadsheet

ASSIGNMENT 1

The following spreadsheet shows rainfall (in millimetres) for the months January to June:

	A	B	C	D	E	F	G
1	RAINFALL RECORD (MM)						
2	1/10/90						
3	ALL						
4	REGIONS	JAN.	FEB.	MARCH	APRIL	MAY	JUNE
5							
6	NORTH	7	9	7	16	12	6
7	WEST	19	16	11	11	7	3
8	SOUTH	3	0	6	3	8	9
9	EAST	7	8	9	10	5	2
10	N-EAST	17	17	15	1	9	5
11	S-EAST	2	2	2	12	4	5
12	N-WEST	12	9	6	13	13	7
13	S-WEST	7	13	15	9	14	15
14							
15							
16							

You are required to type the given data into a spreadsheet, and make the changes below when you have finished. (Make sure when you are typing in the date that this is interpreted by the computer as a label and not a division calculation.)

Carry out the following tasks:

[1] Change the width of column A to twelve characters.

[2] Change the contents of cell A10 to NORTH-EAST, cell A11 to SOUTH-EAST, cell A12 to NORTH-WEST, and cell A13 to SOUTH-WEST.

[3] The rainfall data for February for the East region was incorrectly recorded: it should have been 13 mm. Also, the South-East region data for June is incorrect: it should have been 15 mm. Make the necessary changes.

[4] Delete the contents of cell A3.

[5] Save the spreadsheet as RAIN, and exit the system.

ASSIGNMENT 2

Recall the spreadsheet RAIN.

Carry out the following tasks:

[1] Add a new column between the REGIONS column and the JAN information column (i.e. a new column B). The new information is the area of each region (in square kilometres). The data is as follows:

Regions	Area
North	4768
West	5674
South	3213
East	4356
N-East	675
S-East	567
N-West	453
S-West	689

[2] You will notice that the labels JAN, FEB etc. are not in line with the numbers: the labels are flush left, while the numbers are flush right. Change all month labels and the AREA label so that they are flush right.

[3] Format the rainfall data in the spreadsheet to show one decimal place.

113

[4] Insert a new row of rainfall data for WEST ISLANDS, to be a new row 10; the present row 10 will move down to become row 11, and all other rows below this will also move down automatically. The data for this region is.

Regions	Area	Jan.	Feb.	March	April	May	June
West Islands	345	17	13	19	20	15	12

[5] Format this new rainfall data to one decimal place.

[6] Save the new spreadsheet as NEWRAIN and exit the system.

ASSIGNMENT 3

Recall the spreadsheet NEWRAIN.

Carry out the following tasks:

[1] Add a new column after the JUNE data to show the total rainfall for each of the nine regions. To do this you should use the summation function to add a row of data for each of the regions. The heading for this column should be TOTAL.

[2] Add another column after the TOTAL column to show the average rainfall in each region for the six-month period, using a formula that divides the total rainfall for each region by 6. Call the new column AVERAGE and enter the formulas.

[3] In cell A16 enter the heading TOTAL AREA. In cell B16 show the total area of all the regions; this will be done using the summation function to add the numbers in column B.

[4] Change the date in cell A2 to today's date (make sure it is a label).

[5] Enter your name in cell A3.

[6] Save the spreadsheet as ENDRAIN and exit the system.

ASSIGNMENT 4

This is a simple spreadsheet holding information on students' marks for four assignments. The maximum mark possible for all tests is 10; the minimum possible is 0.

	A	B	C	D	E
1	EXAMINATION RECORD				
2					
3	STUDENT NAME	ASSN 1	ASSN 2	ASSN 3	ASSN 4
4					
5	T OWENS	9	9	7	8
6	S MACDONAGH	0	8	5	4
7	B BURNS	2	7	7	7
8	M PURCELL	9	10	8	7
9	C OWENS	9	7	8	9
10	J POWER	3	6	0	0
11	R EGAN	3	6	5	3
12	L MORGAN	9	10	8	5

You are required to type in the students' names and each exam mark. The total marks and the average marks are calculated using formulas.

Carry out the following tasks:

[1] Set up the given information on a spreadsheet, adjusting column width where necessary and aligning headings on the right.

[2] In column F show the total marks for the four assignments for each student, using a suitable heading.

[3] In column G show the average mark for each student for the four assignments, using a suitable heading. Remember that the average is calculated by dividing the total by the number of assignment tests. (You could use the average function if available on your spreadsheet).

[4] Some marks for assignment 3 have been incorrectly calculated by the teacher: the marks for T. Owens, B. Burns and L. Morgan should all be increased by 2. Make the necessary amendment.

[5] The mark for S. MacDonagh in assignment 4 has been incorrectly recorded: it should be 7. Make the necessary amendment.

[6] In row 14, show the total marks for each assignment, using a suitable heading.

[7] In row 15, show the average mark for each assignment, using a suitable heading.

[8] Save the spreadsheet as EXAMS, and print it.

ASSIGNMENT 5

This is a spreadsheet that shows the sales commission of seven salesmen who sell different products for Annex Ltd. The salesmen are paid their commission at the end of a three-month period.

	A	B	C	D	E	F
1	COMMISSION	ANNEX LTD				
2	DATA					
3	NAME	EE NO.	QTR 1	QTR 2	QTR 3	QTR 4
4						
5	A BEHAN	901	157	295	10	290
6	B COLLINS	064	71	221	130	355
7	C DALY	045	247	242	256	176
8	A NOLAN	256	39	227	64	297
9	A SHIELS	633	142	24	120	241
10	T TIMMONS	908	178	56	67	359
11	J WYNNE	353	335	367	190	186

Carry out the following tasks:

[1] Set up the given spreadsheet.

[2] Change the name C. Daly to C. Davis.

[3] Change the amount for J. Wynne for the second quarter to 153.62.

[4] Change all money amounts to cash format, or at least to display two decimal places.

[5] Delete the contents of the cell in the first column containing the word DATA.

[6] Insert a new column between the employee number (EE NO.) and the first-quarter details to give the following division name for each employee:

A. Behan: Paper

B. Collins: Equipment

C. Daly: Paper

A. Nolan: Paper

A. Shiels: Equipment

T. Timmons: Stationery

J. Wynne: Paper

Use a suitable heading, and make sure the new column is wide enough to accommodate the information.

[7] Set up a new column to show the total commission for each salesman for the four quarters, using a suitable heading.

[8] An end-of-year bonus has been decided on for all salesmen: those in the Paper Division are to get £30 extra; all other divisions get a bonus of £20. Use a suitable column to show this information for all the salesmen.

[9] Add another column to show the total commission plus bonus for each salesman, using a suitable heading.

[10] Add a new row to display the total commission issued in each quarter.

[11] A new salesman (employee number 449) joined the Equipment Division in the third quarter. Insert the following data into the spreadsheet for the third and fourth quarters (making sure that the employee's name is in the proper alphabetical position):

	1st qtr	2nd qtr	3rd qtr	4th qtr
G. Ennis			200	345

[12] Add a new row that shows the average commission issued in each quarter.

[13] A. Nolan is in fact a salesman for the Cork subsidiary company and should not be in this record. Delete this salesman's record.

[14] Save the spreadsheet as COMMISSION.

[15] Copy the column showing the names of the salesmen and the 'total commission plus bonus' column to columns X and Y. Produce a print-out of the contents of columns X and Y *only*.

ASSIGNMENT 6

This spreadsheet is a typical trading profit and loss account for a sole trader.

You are required to set up the spreadsheet, using the appropriate formulas. Note that you will have to change the column width of the first column to accommodate the text.

The figures entered are those that do not require any calculations, i.e. the actual accounting information for that year. The computer should automatically do any of the calculations to sum or deduct in order to calculate the profit.

TRADING PROFIT AND LOSS ACCOUNT
FOR THE YEAR ENDED 31/06/1990

	£	£	£	£
SALES		87300		
LESS SALES RETURNS		4500		82800
LESS COST OF SALES				
OPENING STOCK		7000		
PURCHASES		35000		
COST OF GOODS AVAILABLE		42000		
LESS CLOSING STOCK		10000		32000
GROSS PROFIT				50800
ADD DISCOUNT RECD				450
				51250
LESS EXPENSES				
ESTABLISHMENT				
RENT AND RATES		1786		
ESB		432		
INSURANCE	1500			
LESS INSURANCE PREPAID	200	1300		
DEPRECIATION OFFICE EQUIP	———	659	4177	
ADMINISTRATION				
SALARIES		20000		
OFFICE EXPENSES		569		
POSTAGE		321	20890	
FINANCIAL:				
BAD DEBTS		300		
DIISCOUNT ALLOWED		213		
BANK CHARGES		231	744	
SELLING AND DISTRIBUTION:				
CARRIAGE		500		
MOTOR EXPENSES		1000		
ADVERTISING		3700	5200	31011
NET PROFIT ********				20239

Carry out the following tasks:

[1] Change all figures to cash format, or at least to two decimal places.

[2] The following figures were wrongly entered; make the necessary amendments:
ESB expenses should be £423, not £432.
Purchases should be £45,000.
Motor expenses should be £3,456.

[3] Save this spreadsheet as TRADING.

[4] Type in the new figures for the year ended 31 June 1991, and find the new profit or loss figure. The details are:
Sales: £90,000
Returns: £6,200
Opening stock: £9,200
Purchases: £41,000
Closing stock: £8,000
Discount received: £67
Rent: £2,000
ESB: £500
Insurance: £2,000
Insurance prepaid: £240
Depreciation: £900
Salaries: £35,000
Office expenses: £600
Postage: £400
Bad debts: £200
Discount allowed: £345
Bank charges: £987
Carriage: £210
Motor expenses: £2,645
Advertising: £5,800.

[5] Save the new 1991 trading account as TRADING1, and print the entire spreadsheet.

ASSIGNMENT 7

This is a simple spreadsheet holding information about football league results. The spreadsheet calculates the aggregate points for each team and the total number of games played.

You are required to set up the spreadsheet as shown below, using appropriate formulas and replication.

The information for each team is entered every week, including the number of matches each team has won, lost or drawn so far. The spreadsheet calculates the total number of points gained after each week, and also the total number of games played week after week. The points are calculated on the following basis: win, 3 points; draw, 1 point; lose, 0 points.

FOOTBALL LEAGUE TABLES

TEAM	WON	LOST	DRAW	PLAYED	AUTO POINTS
LIVERPOOL	1			1	3
MANCHESTER		1		1	0
LEEDS			1	1	1
EVERTON		1		1	0
ARSENAL	1			1	3
SPURS			1	1	1

The information already given in the spreadsheet records the results for week 1:
Liverpool beat Manchester
Leeds drew with Spurs
Arsenal beat Everton.

Hint: The points are worked out by adding the number of wins multiplied by 3 to the number of draws multiplied by 1. The losses are not relevant to the auto points. The number of games played is the sum of the number of wins, losses and draws for each team.

Carry out the following tasks:

[1] Save the first week's spreadsheet for the first week as WEEK1.

[2] Exit the system.

[3] Recall the spreadsheet WEEK1 and record the additional information for the second week:
   Liverpool beat Everton (i.e. Liverpool won 2 and Everton lost 2 so far)
   Manchester lost to Arsenal
   Spurs beat Leeds
Note that the number under PLAYED should now be 2 for all.

[4] Save the second week's spreadsheet as WEEK2.

[5] Exit the system.

[6] Recall the spreadsheet WEEK2, and add the following additional data for the third week:
Liverpool beat Spurs
Manchester drew with Arsenal
Everton beat Leeds

[7] Save the third week's spreadsheet as WEEK3, and print this spreadsheet.

ASSIGNMENT 8

This model tabulates the results of any number of questions asked in a survey. In this survey one question is analysed. There are three possible responses: yes (Y), no (N), or maybe (MB).

	A	B	C	D	E	F	G	H	I	J	K	L
1	◄——— DATA INPUT ———►						ANALYSIS					
2	RESPONSE NO.						M	M	M	F	F	F
3		M	F	Y	N	MB	Y	N	MB	Y	N	MB
4	1	1		1			1	0	0	0	0	0
5	2	1		1			1	0	0	0	0	0
6	3		1	1			0	0	0	1	0	0
7	4	1				1	0	0	1	0	0	0
8	5	1		1			1	0	0	0	0	0
9	6	1		1			1	0	0	0	0	0
10	7	1				1	0	0	1	0	0	0
11	8		1		1		0	0	0	0	1	0
12	9		1		1		0	0	0	0	1	0
13	10	1		1			1	0	0	0	0	0
14	11	1		1			1	0	0	0	0	0
15	12	1			1		0	1	0	0	0	0
16	13	1			1		0	1	0	0	0	0
17	14		1			1	0	0	0	0	0	1
18	15	1				1	0	0	1	0	0	0
19	16	1		1			1	0	0	0	0	0
20	17	1		1			1	0	0	0	0	0
21	18	1			1		0	1	0	0	0	0
22	19	1			1		0	1	0	0	0	0
23	20		1		1		0	0	0	0	1	0
24	21		1			1	0	0	0	0	0	1
25	22		1			1	0	0	0	0	0	1
26	23	1				1	0	0	1	0	0	0

Row	Age	M	F	Y	N	MB		M-Y	M-N	M-MB	F-Y	F-N	F-MB
27	24		1	1				0	0	0	1	0	0
28	25	1				1		0	0	1	0	0	0
29	26		1	1				0	0	0	1	0	0
30	27	1				1		0	0	1	0	0	0
31	28	1		1				1	0	0	0	0	0
32	29	1			1			0	1	0	0	0	0
33	30	1				1		0	0	1	0	0	0
34													
35	TOTAL							9	5	6	3	3	4
36													
37													
38	SURVEY ANALYSIS												

		TOTALS			PERCENTAGES			
41		Y	N	MB	Y	N	MB	
42	M	9	5	6	30.0	6.7	20.0	
43	F	3	3	4	10.0	10.0	13.3	
44								
45		12	8	10	40.0	26.7	33.3 =	100%
46	TOTAL	30						
47								
48								
49								

When there is a response a 1 is entered in the DATA INPUT section for yes, no, or maybe. A 1 is also entered under M or F (male or female respondent).

You are required to set up this spreadsheet, using the appropriate formulas and replication. Make sure that column widths are decreased so that more columns can be seen on the screen and page. Save this spreadsheet as SURVEY1.

The only items to be directly entered in this spreadsheet are those under DATA ENTRY: all the other calculations should be made automatically by the computer by the use of formulas.

Carry out the following tasks:

[1] Recall SURVEY1 and enter the following survey results to be analysed, and check your results:

Response no.	Sex	Response
1	Female	Maybe
2	Male	Yes
3	Female	Yes
4	Male	No
5	Male	No
6	Male	No
7	Female	Yes
8	Female	No
9	Male	Maybe
10	Female	No
11	Female	No
12	Female	Maybe
13	Male	Yes
14	Male	Yes
15	Female	Yes
16	Male	Yes
17	Female	No
18	Male	No
19	Female	Yes
20	Male	Maybe
21	Male	No
22	Male	No
23	Female	Yes
24	Male	Maybe
25	Female	No
26	Female	No
27	Male	Yes
28	Female	No
29	Male	No
30	Male	Maybe

[2] Save this new information as SURVEY2.

[3] Print out the statistical information only.

ASSIGNMENT

This spreadsheet is used to keep a record of share prices, so that the progress of the shares can be analysed and compared. The maximum, minimum and average price is calculated for each week. The week change (the difference between the price for the first day of the week and the price for the last day of the week) is calculated, showing the amount of increase or decrease for each week. Finally the three-week data is given.

STOCK EXCHANGE ANALYSIS SHEET
SHARE PRICES FOR

DATE	AIB	BOI	JONES	CRH	CREAN
1/01	3.25	2.00	3.00	1.78	0.89
2/01	3.15	2.10	3.61	1.57	1.22
3/01	3.00	2.10	3.40	1.56	1.34
4/01	2.99	2.10	3.58	1.78	1.78
5/01	3.22	2.58	3.34	1.77	1.56
6/01	3.20	2.58	3.69	1.77	1.76
7/01	3.20	2.57	3.68	1.77	1.45
8/01	3.30	2.45	3.91	1.80	1.67
9/01	3.30	2.34	3.25	1.80	1.56
10/01	3.30	2.67	3.46	1.80	1.56
11/01	3.30	2.44	3.35	1.56	1.67
12/01	3.32	2.44	3.14	1.47	1.76
13/01	3.32	2.45	3.93	1.98	1.32
14/01	3.43	2.33	3.55	2.00	1.32
15/01	3.50	2.33	3.71	2.11	1.01
16/01	3.54	2.33	3.77	2.34	0.99
17/01	3.54	2.33	3.38	2.34	0.98
18/01	3.54	2.33	2.20	2.33	0.90
19/01	3.54	2.33	2.20	2.34	0.89
20/01	3.54	2.33	2.00	2.33	0.88
21/01	3.54	2.33	1.99	2.35	0.97
WEEK 1 HIGH	3.25	2.58	3.69	1.78	1.78
WEEK 1 LOW	2.99	2.00	3.00	1.56	0.89
WEEK 1 AVG.	3.14	2.29	3.47	1.71	1.43
WEEK CHANGE	−0.05	0.57	0.68	−0.01	0.56
WEEK 2 HIGH	3.43	2.67	3.93	2.00	1.76
WEEK 2 LOW	3.30	2.33	3.14	1.47	1.32
WEEK 2 AVG.	3.32	2.45	3.51	1.77	1.55
WEEK CHANGE	0.13	−0.12	−0.37	0.20	−0.35
WEEK 3 HIGH	3.54	2.33	3.77	2.35	1.32
WEEK 3 LOW	3.43	2.33	1.99	2.00	0.88
WEEK 3 AVG.	3.52	2.33	2.85	2.27	0.99
WEEK CHANGE	0.11	0.00	−1.56	0.35	−0.35
3-WEEK HIGH	3.54	2.67	3.93	2.35	1.78
3-WEEK LOW	2.99	2.00	1.99	1.47	0.88
3-WEEK AVG.	3.33	2.36	3.25	1.93	1.31
3-WEEK CHANGE	0.29	0.33	−1.01	0.57	0.08

You are required to set up the spreadsheet as given, using the appropriate formulas and replication (use the 'minimum' and 'maximum' functions).

The only items to be directly entered in this spreadsheet are the financial data for each share entered daily: all the other calculations should be made automatically by the computer.

Carry out the following tasks:

[1] Plot the data for the three weeks for AIB, using a line graph on paper or using the graphing facility on your computer if available.

[2] Plot the three-week average for each share, using a bar graph.

[3] Obtain extra data from the daily papers to expand the model to allow for ten different companies.

[4] Fix the row containing the company name headings so that it does not scroll off the screen when you are moving down the spreadsheet.

[5] Produce a print-out of the three-week information only.

[6] Save the spreadsheet as SHARES, and print out the entire spreadsheet.

ASSIGNMENT 10

Interest for one year is found by using the formula:

$$I = \frac{P \times R}{100}$$

where P = principal and R = rate

Remember that with simple interest the principal is the same every year, and therefore the interest is also the same. Compound interest is calculated on a different principal each year, which includes the interest of the previous years. For example, to find the compound interest and simple interest on £100 for two years at 8 per cent:

Simple interest		Compound interest	
Year 1	(100 x 8) ÷ 100 = 8	(100 x 8) ÷ 100 = 8	
Year 2	(100 x 8) ÷ 100 = 8	(108 x 8) ÷ 100 = 8.64	
Totals (interest)	£16	£16.64	

You are required to set up the spreadsheet shown below, which gives the simple interest and principal for twenty years, using the appropriate formulas and relative or absolute replication. Make sure that all money amounts are in cash format.

	A	B	C	D	E	F	G
1		COMPOUND VERSUS SIMPLE INTEREST					
2							
3		PRINCIPAL	£150.00				
4		YEAR	1990				
5		RATE (%)	9				
6							
7							
8		SIMPLE	SIMPLE	TOTAL	COMPOUND	COMPOUND	TOT./COMPD
9	YEAR	PRINCIPAL	INTEREST	INTEREST	PRINCIPAL	INTEREST	INTEREST
10							
11	1990	£150.00	£13.50	£13.50	£150.00	£13.50	£13.50
12	1991	£150.00	£13.50	£27.00	£163.50	£14.72	£28.22
13	1992	£150.00	£13.50	£40.50	£178.22	£16.04	£44.25
14	1993	£150.00	£13.50	£54.00	£194.25	£17.48	£61.74
15	1994	£150.00	£13.50	£67.50	£211.74	£19.06	£80.79
16	1995	£150.00	£13.50	£81.00	£230.79	£20.77	£101.57
17	1996	£150.00	£13.50	£94.50	£251.57	£22.64	£124.21
18	1997	£150.00	£13.50	£108.00	£274.21	£24.68	£148.88
19	1998	£150.00	£13.50	£121.50	£298.88	£26.90	£175.78
20	1999	£150.00	£13.50	£135.00	£325.78	£29.32	£205.10
21	2000	£150.00	£13.50	£148.50	£355.10	£31.96	£237.06
22	2001	£150.00	£13.50	£162.00	£387.06	£34.84	£271.90
23	2002	£150.00	£13.50	£175.50	£421.90	£37.97	£309.87
24	2003	£150.00	£13.50	£189.00	£459.87	£41.39	£351.26
25	2004	£150.00	£13.50	£202.50	£501.26	£45.11	£396.37
26	2005	£150.00	£13.50	£216.00	£546.37	£49.17	£445.55
27	2006	£150.00	£13.50	£229.50	£595.55	£53.60	£499.15
28	2007	£150.00	£13.50	£243.00	£649.15	£58.42	£557.57
29	2008	£150.00	£13.50	£256.50	£707.57	£63.68	£621.25
30	2009	£150.00	£13.50	£270.00	£771.25	£69.41	£690.66
31	2010	£150.00	£13.50	£283.50	£840.66	£75.66	£766.32
32							

Hint: The TOTAL SIMPLE INTEREST column accumulates interest. In the first year this will be the same as the SIMPLE INTEREST amount. The formula in cell D11 will be +C11; in the second year it will be the previous total plus the simple interest of the second year. The formula in cell D12 will be +D11+C12. This can then be copied down column D using relative cell references. The same procedure can be used to accumulate other columns of data.

The only items to be directly entered in this spreadsheet are the year, principal, and interest rate: all the other calculations should be made automatically by the computer.

Carry out the following tasks:

[1] Using the example, show what the compound and simple interest would be on £300 at 13 per cent invested in 1990 for fifteen years.

[2] Using the example, show what the compound and simple interest would be on £250 at 11.13 per cent invested in 1990 for sixteen years.

[3] Which of the following two investments gives the greater interest: £1,050 at 12 per cent for five years' compound interest or £1,200 at 12 per cent for five years' simple interest?

[4] Add a new column to your spreadsheet after the TOTAL COMPOUND INTEREST column to show the difference between simple and compound interest for each year. Use a suitable heading.

[5] If the difference between simple and compound interest on a sum of money for two years at 6 per cent is £36, find the sum.

[6] If the difference between simple and compound interest on a sum of money for ten years at 9 per cent is £38.50, find the sum.

[7] Save the spreadsheet as INTEREST, and print it out.

ASSIGNMENT 11

Depreciation is the cost of wear and tear to a business on assets that it owns. This cost tends to vary from year to year, depending on the method of depreciation used. The method used here is the 'declining balance'. This is similar to the concept of compound interest, except that the value of the goods is reducing all the time. For example:

Asset: car

Cost: £1,000

Number of years of life: 3

Rate of depreciation: 10 per cent

Year	£ Depreciation	£ Cumulative deprecation	£ Net book value
1	100 (1,000 × 0.1)	100	900 (1,000–100)
2	90 (900 × 0.1)	190 (100 + 90)	810 (1,000–190)
3	81 (810 × 0.1)	271 (190 + 81)	729 (1,000–271)

You are required to set up the spreadsheet shown below, using appropriate formulas and relative and absolute replication, and to save this spreadsheet as DEPREC1.

The only items to be directly entered in this spreadsheet are the asset, year, cost, and depreciation rate: all the other calculations should be made automatically by the computer.

	A	B	C	D
1				
2		DEPRECIATION SOLUTION		
3				
4	ITEM	IBM PC		
5	YEAR	1989		
6	YEARS	10		
7	COST	£1000.00		
8				
9	RATE (%)	25		
10				
11	YEAR	DEPRECIATION	CUMULATIVE	NET BOOK VALUE
12				
13	1989	£250.00	£250.00	£750.00
14	1990	£187.50	£437.50	£562.50
15	1991	£140.63	£578.13	£421.88
16	1992	£105.47	£683.59	£316.41
17	1993	£79.10	£762.70	£237.30
18	1994	£59.33	£822.02	£177.98
19	1995	£44.49	£866.52	£133.48
20	1996	£33.37	£899.89	£100.11
21	1997	£25.03	£924.92	£75.08
22	1998	£18.77	£943.69	£56.31
23	1999	£14.08	£957.76	£42.24
24	2000	£10.56	£968.32	£31.68
25	2001	£7.92	£976.24	£23.76
26	2002	£5.94	£982.18	£17.82
27	2003	£4.45	£986.64	£13.36
28	2004	£3.34	£989.98	£10.02
29	2005	£2.51	£992.48	£7.52

Carry out the following tasks:

[1] Show the depreciation details for the following asset by recalling DEPREC1 and changing the variable information. No formulas should be changed. Save this new information as DEPREC2.

> Item: Ford Escort van
> Year: 1990
> Cost: £6,000
> Estimated life: five years
> Depreciation rate: 23.89 per cent

[2] Recall DEPREC2 and add a new row 8 (between the rows containing cost and rate) to show scrap value.

[3] Get the computer to calculate the rate of depreciation rather than having it as an input, by using the following formula:

$$\text{Rate of depreciation} = 1 - \left(\frac{S}{C}\right)^{\frac{1}{n}}$$

where n = the number of years of life of the asset, S = the scrap value, and C = the cost. This formula will be entered in the RATE cell (B9) as $1-((scrap/cost)^{(1/years)})$.

[4] Produce a print-out of the spreadsheet showing the details for the following asset, using the new automatic rate, and save the spreadsheet as DEPREC3:

> Item: autoprinter
> Year: 1990
> Estimated life: eight years
> Cost: £40,000
> Scrap value: £5,000

Note: After the eighth year the scrap value will be equal to the net book value in that year.

ASSIGNMENT 12

This spreadsheet shows a simple profit and loss statement for a given year. The other profit and loss statements are predicted figures based on this year's figures and assumed percentage increase or decrease trends. These figures would be worked out using past accounts and future trends.

PREDICTED PERCENTAGE	PROFIT AND LOSS PROJECTION		
	YEAR	ACTUAL 1990	PROJECTED 1991
0.1	SALES	£220,000.00	£200,000.00
0.05	RETURNS	£18,000.00	£18,900.00
	NET SALES	£182,000.00	£201,100.00
	LESS COSTS		
0.22	LIGHT, HEAT	£20,000.00	£24,400.00
− 0.4	ADMINISTRATION	£10,000.00	£6,000.00
0.11	MATERIALS	£70,000.00	£77,700.00
− 0.32	WAGES	£40,000.00	£27,200.00
	TOTAL	£140,000.00	£135,300.00
	PROFIT	£42,000.00	£65,800.00

PROJECTED 1992	PROJECTED 1993	PROJECTED 1994	PROJECTED 1995
£242,000.00	£266,200.00	£292,820.00	£322,102.00
£19,845.00	£20,837.25	£21,879.11	£22,973.07
£222,155.00	£245,362.75	£270,940.89	£299,128.93
£29,768.00	£36,316.96	£44,306.69	£54,054.16
£3,600.00	£2,160.00	£1,296.00	£777.60
£86,247.00	£95,734.17	£160,420.17	£117,954.07
£18,496.00	£12,577.28	£110,520.72	£5,815.73
£138,111.00	£146,788.41	£160,420.17	£178,601.57
£84,044.00	£98,574.34	£110,520.72	£120,527.36

You are required to set up this spreadsheet, using appropriate formulas (on screen the spreadsheet will have projected 1992–95 figures in the columns to the right of the 1991 figures). Replicate the 1990 figures up to the year 1995, using relative and absolute replication. Note that in the PREDICTED PERCENTAGE column the 10 per cent increase is shown as +0.1, the 40 per cent decrease is shown as –0.4, and so on.

The only items to be directly entered in this spreadsheet are the actual first-year figures (1990) and the percentages: all the other calculations should be made automatically by the computer.

Carry out the following tasks:

[1] Make sure to change all cash amounts to money format or at least to two decimal places.

[2] What would the new profit or loss be in 1995 if the predicted trend in sales was a 22 per cent increase? Make a note of this new figure on paper.

[3] Change all percentages by 1 per cent. What is the new profit in 1994?

[4] Insert a new row to include overtime as an expense, with a 1990 figure of £5,600 and an assumed increase of 3.2 per cent (to be shown as +0.032).

[5] What would the new profit or loss be in 1995 if the following percentages are predicted?
 5 per cent increase in sales
 2 per cent decrease in returns
 3.24 per cent increase in light and heat costs
 2.22 per cent decrease in administration costs
 1 per cent increase in materials costs
 10 per cent increase in wages
 4 per cent decrease in overtime

[6] The expense for administration has been wrongly included in this set of accounts. Delete the appropriate row from the spreadsheet.

[7] Save the final spreadsheet as PROJECT.

ASSIGNMENT 13

A spreadsheet allows a railway line to receive bookings for particular trains. The following is some information relating to ticket codes and prices:

Ticket type:	First class	Second class	Standard	Economy
Ticket code:	1	2	3	4
Basic price:	£75	£60	£50	£45

The following groups have booked a particular train to Galway:

Travel group	Ticket type	Group numbers
Club	1	10
JWT	4	20
Tiglin	3	25
Adventure Co.	2	42
Gael-Linn	4	40
YMCA	4	4

You are required to enter the above information in a spreadsheet.

The only items to be directly entered in this spreadsheet are the ticket code (or price, if you are not using the 'look-up' function) and the number in the group: all the other calculations should be made automatically by the computer. Standard data such as ticket price, penalty amounts etc. should, where necessary, be changeable without changing formulas.

Carry out the following tasks:

[1] Using suitable headings and formulas, show the following information for each of the above groups:

Cash receipts: the price of the ticket multiplied by the number booked by the travel agents. (Use the 'look-up' function; if this is not available do not use a ticket code but enter the price of the ticket as an input in the TICKET TYPE column.)

Group discount: If there are twenty-five or more people in a group booking for a particular type of ticket then a 10 per cent discount is given on the basic ticket price (use the 'if' function).

Cash receipts less discounts.

VAT: 10 per cent of total cash receipts less group discount for each booking.

Penalty: If the cash receipts from any group are less than or equal to £900 then an additional surcharge of £10 is applied (use the 'if' function).

Total charge to each group: includes cash receipt, penalty charges if any, VAT, and deducted discount.

[2] A warning should be given if more than 150 passengers are booked on the train (use the 'if' function).

[3] Set up a simple profit and loss statement for the data, showing total revenue excluding VAT and the profit, given that the following expenses are incurred:

Fuel: £170.00
Wages: £140.00
Administration: £134.44

[4] Save the spreadsheet as TRAIN.

[5] Print the entire spreadsheet.

[6] Produce a print-out of the profit and loss statement only.

ASSIGNMENT 14

A spreadsheet shows information on a computer company that sells five products, which are coded 1 to 5. The spreadsheet is used for processing orders and for calculating amounts due. It also accumulates sales figures for these products.

The following are the prices and costs of the computer products on sale:

Product:	IBM PS2 30	Macintosh LC	Amstrad PC3286	Macintosh Classic	Commodore Amiga
Code:	1	2	3	4	5
Price:	£2,375	£1,590	£1,379	£995	£609
Cost price:	£1,781	£1,193	£1,034	£746	£457

The following orders were received:

Customer name	Product code	Quantity order
Computech	1	20
Bytes	1	10
Futura	1	8
Videomart	2	4
Computer Centre	1	14
Electron	4	22
Technocom	5	10
PC World	2	10
Microshop	3	10

You are required to set up the spreadsheet, entering the above data for each order and showing the required information, using the appropriate formulas and replication.

The only items to be directly entered in this spreadsheet are the customer name, product codes, and quantity ordered: all the other calculations should be made automatically by the computer.

The following information needs to be shown for each customer:

First price: the price multiplied by quantity ordered (use the 'look-up' function if available).

Discount: If fifteen or more are ordered there is a 10 per cent discount on the first price; otherwise there is no discount.

Total cost: the cost multiplied by the quantity ordered (use the 'look-up' function if available; if not, enter the actual prices).

VAT (21 per cent): calculated as a percentage of the first price less discount.

Total due: the first price less discount, plus VAT.

Sales analysis: Five analysis columns are required, one for each product. These columns accumulate the 'total due' for product codes 1 to 5; for example, if all the orders were for product 1 only the product 1 analysis column would have numbers in it. (Use the 'if' function.)

Carry out the following tasks:

[1] Show in an appropriate area of the spreadsheet the average amount due for each of the nine customers.

[2] Insert a new column to show the actual date of each order.

[3] Show in an appropriate area of the spreadsheet the total profit (the first price less discounts and total costs).

[4] Save the spreadsheet as SALES.

[5] Print the entire spreadsheet.

ASSIGNMENT 15

This spreadsheet allows the wages of individual employees to be broken down into the minimum number of notes and coins required. It also totals the number of notes and coins needed for a particular wage run. This procedure is often called 'wage payment analysis'.

WAGE ANALYSIS

NAME	AMOUNT	£50.00	£20.00	£10.00	£5.00	£1.00	£0.50	£0.20	£0.10	£0.05	£0.02	£0.01
C KEARNEY	£256.36	5	0	0	1	1	0	1	1	1	0	1
P MAHER	£326.59	6	1	0	1	1	1	0	0	1	1	1
T KEARNEY	£0.13	0	0	0	0	0	0	0	1	0	1	0
P HORGAN	£112.21	2	0	1	0	2	0	1	0	0	0	0
D MAHER	£11.00	0	0	1	0	1	0	0	0	0	0	0
L MAHER	£445.70	8	2	0	1	0	1	0	1	1	2	0
P FOSTER	£211.00	4	0	1	0	1	0	0	0	0	0	0
R LYNCH	£200.00	4	0	0	0	0	0	0	0	0	0	0
D DEVLIN	£567.00	11	0	1	1	2	0	0	0	0	0	0
J JOYCE	£567.90	11	0	1	1	2	1	1	1	1	2	0
J DALTON	£567.87	11	0	1	1	2	1	1	1	1	1	0
S DOYLE	£567.87	11	0	1	1	2	1	1	1	1	1	0
S SLANE	£567.87	11	0	1	1	2	1	1	1	1	1	0
L CORR	£0.02	0	0	0	0	0	0	0	0	0	1	0
F LEAVY	£54.67	1	0	0	0	4	1	0	1	1	1	0
A BYRNE	£45.23	0	2	0	1	0	0	1	0	0	1	0
P KENNY	£456.00	9	0	0	1	1	0	0	0	0	0	0
K MURPHY	£343.67	6	2	0	0	3	1	0	1	1	1	0
A MORRIS	£98.09	1	2	0	1	3	0	0	0	1	2	0
S BYRNE	£454.21	9	0	0	0	4	0	1	0	0	0	0
S ALLEN	£123.00	2	1	0	0	3	0	0	0	0	0	0
C MORGAN	£234.00	4	1	1	0	4	0	0	0	0	0	0
J COLLINS	£234.00	4	1	1	0	4	0	0	0	0	0	0
A HANLEY	£789.00	15	1	1	1	4	0	0	0	0	0	0
D BROWNE	£34.98	0	1	1	0	4	1	2	0	1	1	0
H SMITH	£34.98	0	1	1	0	4	1	2	0	1	1	0
N BISHOP	£234.65	4	1	1	0	4	1	0	1	1	0	0
S KEARNEY	£34.98	0	1	1	0	4	1	2	0	1	1	0
R MORGAN	£34.90	0	1	1	0	4	1	1	1	1	2	0
K FOSTER	£234.98	4	1	1	0	4	1	2	0	1	1	0
TOTAL		143	19	17	12	70	14	17	11	16	21	2

You are required to set up the spreadsheet as given, using the appropriate formulas and replication. Allow for at least twenty employees.

The only items to be directly entered in this spreadsheet are the employee name and actual net wage: all the other calculations should be made automatically by the computer.

Hint: To divide, for example, £235 into the minimum number of notes, you would go through the following procedure:

The number of £50 notes = 235 ÷ 50 = 4.7; find the integer of this number (use the 'integer' function): 4 is the number required.

The number of £20 notes = (*remainder* [235] – (4 × 50)) ÷ 20 = 1.75; find the integer: 1 is the number required.

The number of £10 notes = (*last remainder* [35] – (1 × 20)) ÷ 10 = 1.5; find the integer: 1 is the number required.

The number of £5 notes = (*last remainder* [15] – (1 × 10)) ÷ 5 = 1; find the integer: 1 is the number required.

And so on. You will need additional columns to calculate the remainders, and these can be put anywhere in the spreadsheet.

Carry out the following tasks:

[1] Experiment with different figures to check that your calculations are correct.

[2] Copy the names from the first column to the last column, using the 'copy' function.

[3] Save the spreadsheet as COIN, and print it.

Chapter 7

Spreadsheet concepts

This chapter will cover the following concepts:

1. Numeric bias
2. Practical limitations
3. Data files
4. Number format
5. Spreadsheet applications
6. Manual versus computerised spreadsheets
7. Advantages of spreadsheets
8. Limitations of spreadsheets

1. Numeric bias

The main function of a spreadsheet is to carry out mathematical calculations. Numeric cells can be linked and manipulated by means of formulas. The relationship between one cell and another is most relevant where numbers are concerned: text plays no part in the calculations (other than in the form of labels), and cannot be mathematically manipulated. Textual data is best manipulated by a data-base program, because it assigns value to text by the use of indexing (see the data-base chapters for more details). This allows for alphabetical sorts and searches.

2. Practical limitations

Unlike other types of program, spreadsheets require that all the data be in the internal memory of the computer before it is manipulated. This is because of the nature of spreadsheet operations: for example, the formula +B6*A999 requires that the spreadsheet have immediate access to the contents of cells B6 and A999. This immediate access is only possible from the internal memory (RAM) of the computer.

In some spreadsheets the changing of one number can generate thousands of changes in other cells. These other cells must be immediately accessible to permit rapid calculation. Thus the size of the internal memory will determine the maximum size of the spreadsheet. Most large spreadsheets have millions of available cells, but only a fraction of the spreadsheet can be used, because of the memory size.

3. Data files

To run a spreadsheet, a suitable program must be loaded into the computer so that it will be able to set up a blank spreadsheet and make all the various functions work. The components of this program are the **program files**.

If you save typed-in data, including labels, numbers, and formulas, this information will be recorded as **data files**. The program files allow you to perform calculations and instructions on the data files.

4. Number format

The numbers in a spreadsheet can be displayed in a number of ways.

Integer format

A number is in integer format when it consists of an integer or whole number only, i.e. when it does not include any decimal fraction.

Real format

A number is in real format when it includes a decimal fraction.

Cash format

A number is in cash format when it includes two decimal places and usually also has a thousand marker (comma or space) where necessary; it may also have a pound sign in front of it.

Exponent format

A number is in exponent format (also called 'standard index form' or 'scientific notation') when it is displayed in the form of a real number between 1 and 9 multiplied by 10 to the power of the appropriate integer: this saves space in the display of very large (or very small) numbers. The general form is

$$[real\ number] \times 10\,n$$
where n is the exponent, but in computer usage this is displayed as
$$[real\ number]\ en$$

Examples:
$285,000,000 = 2.85e8$ (i.e. 2.85×10^8)
$0.000285 = 2.85e{-}4$ (i.e. 2.85×10^{-4})

A **rounding error** is the difference between the correct number and the displayed number. This usually occurs when a number has many decimal places. For example, if $2.8545e2$ is displayed as 285.5, what is the rounding error? Solution:

Displayed number	285.50
Correct number	285.45
Rounding error	+000.05

5. Spreadsheet applications

The following are only a selection of the many practical uses to which computer spreadsheets may be put.

Financial applications

- Depreciation schedules, showing year depreciation, cumulative depreciation, and net book value
- Production of invoices and statements
- Currency exchange rates, where the various currencies are entered and the other currency equivalents are displayed
- Tax tables and forms showing PAYE calculations and totals, for example the tax deduction card for an employee
- Compound and simple interest schedules for investment evaluations
- Loan repayment schedules, including mortgage repayments, showing the best options and tax relief
- Car financing evaluation, to determine the best choice between hire, lease and hire-purchase for a given set of variables

Non-financial applications

- Student marks record, including marks for examinations taken and a full statistical analysis for each student, examination, and class
- Football league tables
- Mathematical evaluations, using different mathematical and scientific formulas

Analysis and projection applications

- Projection of yearly accounts based on predicted percentage increases or decreases
- Predicting future value of investments
- Predicting minimum stock levels and reorder levels based on past stock and sales records
- Statistical analysis of research data, including averages, standard deviations, correlation coefficients, and graphic analysis

6. Manual versus computerised spreadsheets

Spreadsheets are not a new idea: similar forms drawn up on large sheets of paper have been used for hundreds of years for tabulating calculations. It is useful to compare the two systems.

Function	Computerised	Manual
Editing	Easy: changes can be made easily, either while data is being typed in or afterwards, by using the 'delete' or 'type over' and other editing functions	Difficult to delete or change data, as it is 'fixed'
Updating	Easy: 'insert' or 'add on' facility	Can be difficult
Recalculation	Possible: just type in new data	Need to set up a new spreadsheet
Automatic calculation	Possible	Not possible
Extension	Possible: limited by size of RAM	Possible: limited by paper size
Replication	Possible at different levels: relative or absolute	Not possible
Speed of use	Fast	Slow
When used	Where there is changeable data, i.e. needing regular editing or new calculations	Where data is fixed, i.e. where data is only calculated once
	Where speed of calculation is important	Where data is analysed in different places
	Most types of application	Where data collected and used in the field may not be suitable for computer use

7. Advantages of spreadsheets

Some of the advantages of computer spreadsheets can be summarised as follows:

1. Calculations that would be very repetitive if carried out manually can be done with ease by the facility to copy or replicate formulas.

2. If one item in a spreadsheet is changed, all the other figures relating to it automatically change. This allows the user to experiment with different figures to test policy or rate changes. These 'what if' calculations allow for better and speedier decision-making.

3. Spreadsheets can be easily edited with the aid of the insert, delete and formatting facilities.

4. Many built-in mathematical, statistical and financial functions are available for calculation purposes.

5. Data stored can be quickly accessed.

6. Parts or all the spreadsheet can be printed.

7. The use of 'integrated packages' allows spreadsheet information to be transferred to other application programs, such as graphics and word-processing, for presentation purposes.

8. Limitations of spreadsheets

Some of the disadvantages of computer spreadsheets can be summarised as follows:

1. Care must be taken when replicating a formula, as one mistake in the original formula will be repeated in all the copied formulas.

2. Spreadsheet size is limited by the capacity of the computer's RAM. Memory capacity can be quickly consumed where many formulas are used.

3. Computers are expensive when they are used for a one-off analysis.

4. Staff must be trained to enter and edit spreadsheets.

5. Only a fraction of the spreadsheet can be seen at any time.

Questions

Multi-choice questions

1. Which of the following is not a facility of a spreadsheet?
   - (a) copying
   - (b) deleting data
   - (c) sorting data
   - (d) quick cursor movement

2. A column is—
   - (a) a horizontal series of cells
   - (b) any non-numeric data
   - (c) a vertical series of cells
   - (d) a block of cells?

3. If the formula +A34*C23 is copied down one cell using relative cell references, which of the following will the new formula be?
   - (a) +B34*D23
   - (b) +B35*D24
   - (c) +A35*C24
   - (d) +A34*C23

4. If the number 22.854 is displayed on a spreadsheet as 22.86, what is the rounding error:

  (a) 0.04
  (b) 0.06
  (c) 0.004
  (d) 0.006?

5. When a cell reference does not change when copied, it is called—

  (a) relative
  (b) automatic
  (c) fixed
  (d) absolute?

6. Replication means:

  (a) to sum a block of cells
  (b) the use of a formula many times
  (c) copying the contents of a cell or cells to another cell or cells
  (d) changing the format of a cell?

7. An absolute cell reference means:

  (a) that the cell reference changes when copied
  (b) that the cell reference is absolutely correct
  (c) that the cell reference does not change when copied
  (d) that the result in the cell will remain the same?

8. 'What if?' calculation means:

  (a) one that uses the 'logical if' function
  (b) asking a question
  (c) replicating formulas
  (d) experimenting with different numbers to see different results?

9. Which of the following numbers is in real format?

  (a) 20
  (b) 32.14
  (c) 2.85e3
  (d) $2.34*10^6$

10. Which of the following is not a suitable spreadsheet application?

  (a) tax tables
  (b) a telephone directory
  (c) statistical analysis of data
  (d) projection of accounts

Short-answer questions

  1. Describe briefly what a spreadsheet looks like.
  2. Name the three types of data that can be entered in a cell.
  3. What is the most useful facility or function of a spreadsheet?
  4. Give three examples of a non-financial spreadsheet.

5. Spreadsheets are extremely useful analytical tools but should be used with caution. Explain this statement.
6. Give an example of an application that would be better done on a manual spreadsheet than a computerised spreadsheet.
7. Give two examples of 'what if?' calculations.
8. What are built-in functions? List four built-in functions available on your spreadsheet.
9. How many available cells has a spreadsheet program with 300 columns and 4,000 rows? Can all of these cells be used on all computers?
10. Why is it not possible to see all the spreadsheet at one time, and what functions compensate for this?

Glossary of spreadsheet terms

absolute cell reference: a cell reference that does not adjust or change when a formula is copied to another cell.

alignment: the cell formatting function that controls the position of labels within a cell.

automatic recalculation mode: a feature whereby cell values are recalculated every time any cell relating to these values is changed.

block: a series of adjacent cells manipulated as an entity; also called a 'range'.

built-in functions: ready-to-use formulas that perform mathematical, statistical and logical calculations, for example the summation function.

cash format: a value format in which a number is displayed with two decimal places and usually with a pound sign and thousand markers.

cell: a rectangle formed by the intersection of a row and a column and in which numbers, labels and formulas can be entered and edited.

cell address: a code used to identify a cell by specifying the row and column, for example B34.

cell format: the way in which values and labels are displayed in a cell; the more common formats for numbers include integer format, cash format, and exponent format; common formats for labels are flush right, flush left, and centred.

cell pointer: a rectangular highlight that indicates the current cell, in the same way that the cursor indicates the current position in text.

cell reference: a cell address when used in a formula, for example A1 and A10 in the formula @SUM(A1..A10).

cell type: the classification of a cell according to whether it contains a label, a value, or a formula.

centred: a label format in which the text is half way between the left and right edges of the column.

column: a vertical series of cells running the full length of the spreadsheet, and usually identified by a letter or letters.

exponent format: a value format in which a number is displayed in the form of a real number between 1 and 9 multiplied by 10 to the power of the appropriate integer.

flush left: a label format in which the text is aligned with the left-hand edge of the column.

flush right: a label format in which the text is aligned with the right-hand edge of the column.

formula: an algebraic expression that defines the relationship between two or more values, using cell references to represent the values or formulas they contain, for example +A2+B7.

integer format: a value format in which a number has no decimal fraction.

non-scrolling titles: a function that allows rows or columns to remain fixed on the display when the rest of the screen scrolls out of view; also called 'fixed titles'.

label: any non-numeric data in the spreadsheet.

real format: a value format in which a number includes a decimal fraction.

relative cell reference: a cell reference that is adjusted or changed when a formula is copied to another cell.

replication: the function that allows labels, values and formulas to be copied to another part of the spreadsheet (also called 'copying').

rounding error: the difference between the exact number and the displayed number.

row: a horizontal series of cells running across the full breath of the spreadsheet, and usually identified by a number.

spreadsheet: a screen image of a form or matrix made up of rows and columns in which automatic and interconnected calculations are made.

spreadsheet program: the computer program needed to set up a spreadsheet and to allow the use of commands, formulas, and special functions.

value: any arithmetic quantity in the spreadsheet.

'what if?' analysis: the manipulation of data so that numeric variables are changed to show the effect of different policies.

window: a rectangular frame in the display that allows other parts of the spreadsheet to be viewed on the same screen.

Section D

Word-processing

Chapter 8

Introduction to word-processing

A word-processor is a program that makes it possible to use a microcomputer for entering, storing and manipulating text.

In typing a document we usually make some mistakes: spelling errors, missing or duplicated words, and paragraphs in the wrong order, or even omitted. A word-processor allows us to correct these errors and to make any other changes before the document is printed. It also allows us to store a copy of the document onto disk and to recall it later and edit it as required.

In this chapter we will examine the following facilities of a word-processor:
1. Elementary editing: deleting and inserting
2. More advanced editing: moving text
3. Enhancing the appearance of a document
4. The 'find and replace' facility
5. Setting tabs
6. Stored paragraphs
7. Merge printing

1. Elementary editing: deleting and inserting

Patrick Matthews is secretary to the managing director of a company that manufactures building insulation: Cavityfoam Enterprises Ltd. He produces all documents on his microcomputer, which is equipped with a word-processor program.

This is the first draft of a document describing the company and its products:

Cavityfoam Enterprises Ltd was founded in 1981 by John Hall and Fionnuala O'Connor. The aim of the company was to produce good-quality home insulation products at a competitive price.

The company initially employed only twelve people. As markets were quickly established, the number of people employed by the firm grew rapidly. In 1985 the company employed forty-three people, and by 1990 the workforce numbered seventy-eight.

In response to a need in the market, the company directors decided to branch into factory farm building insulation products. John Hall spent nine months in Toronto observing the mannufacture and testing of Canadian insulation products.

Today Cavityfoam enterprises Ltd is one of Ireland's leading companies in the manufacture of insulation building products. The Company employs 265 people, and last year's profits were £1.7 million.

Fionnuala now edits this first draft. There are standard ways of indicating what changes are to be made; the most important of these are shown here:

Cavityfoam Enterprises Ltd was founded in 1981 by John Hall and Fionnuala O'Connor. The aim of the company was to produce good-quality home insulation products at a competitive price.

The company initially employed ⒶonlЧ twelve people. As markets were quickly established, the number of people employed by theⒷfirm grew rapidly. In 1985 the company employed forty-three people, and by 1990 the workⒸforce numbered seventy-eight.

In response to a need in the market, the company directors decided to branch into factoryⒹ and farm building insulation products. John Hall spent nine months in Toronto observing the manⒺufacture and testing of Canadian insulation products.

Today Cavityfoam Ⓕenterprises Ltd is one of Ireland's leading companies in the manufacture of Ⓖ|insulation|building|products. TheⒽⓗompany ⒽEmploys 265 people, and last year's profits were Ⓙ£1.7 million.

A Delete a word
B Substitute a word
C Insert a space between words
D Insert a character or word
E Delete a character
F Change from lower case (ordinary letters) to capitals
G Transpose (swap) words
H Change from capitals to lower case
J Close up (remove a space)

New text can be inserted into a document by moving the cursor to the correct position and simply typing the text. Unwanted text can be deleted by positioning the cursor at the appropriate place and giving one of the delete commands. Word-processors have commands to delete a character, word, line, or block of text.

Most word-processors will rearrange the text after you have edited a line so that the remainder of the text will move forwards or back to fill the space.

The corrected text will now appear as follows:

Cavityfoam Enterprises Ltd was founded in 1981 by John Hall and Fionnuala O'Connor. The aim of the company was to produce good-quality home insulation products at a competitive price.

The company initially employed twelve people. As markets were quickly established, the number of people employed by the company grew rapidly. In 1985 the company employed forty-three people, and by 1990 the work force numbered seventy-eight.

In response to a need in the market, the company directors decided to branch into factory and farm building insulation products. John Hall spent nine months in Toronto observing the manufacture and testing of Canadian insulation products.

Today Cavityfoam Enterprises Ltd is one of Ireland's leading companies in the manufacture of building insulation products. The company employs 265 people, and last year's profits were £1.7 million.

2. More advanced editing: moving text

The managing director has asked Patrick to draw up a letter to the wholesalers who stock Cavity-foam products. The letter should tell them of future price increases on some products and of the development of a new insulation material suitable for bungalows. Here is his draft:

Dear wholesaler,

We regret to inform you that, because of spiralling raw material costs, we have increased the price of some products. Our very popular Astrofoam has been increased from £11.75 to £12.50 per cubic metre. Our insulation foam for farm buildings, Agrifoam, has been increased from £8.50 to £9.20 per cubic metre. The company has decided to extend its guarantee from ten to fifteen years on all of its insulation products. This fact should be made clear to the retailers, as our largest competitors only guarantee their products for seven years.

We are introducing a new insulation product called Bungafoam onto the market. This is suitable for bungalows, and is competitively priced at £11.50 per cubic metre.

Our sales representative will be calling on you on 28 March. He will furnish you with all the details of our other insulation products and will accept your order this month.

I wish to remind you of our 5 per cent discount on all products that are paid for in full on the delivery date.

I am confident that you will continue to stock the Cavityfoam range of insulation products.

Yours faithfully,

Fionnuala O'Connor
Managing Director

Fionnuala feels that some changes need to be made to this letter.

- Paragraph 2 should be moved so that it becomes the first paragraph of the letter. This is achieved by marking the paragraph to be moved and positioning the cursor at the new position in the document. The command to move a marked block of text must then be given.

- One paragraph should be divided into two. The paragraph that starts 'We regret to inform you…' should be split at the point that begins 'The company has decided to extend…' This is achieved by inserting two carriage returns (pressing the 'enter' key twice) at the appropriate position in the text.

- Two separate paragraphs should be joined together. The paragraph that starts 'Our sales representative will be calling…' and the one that starts 'I wish to remind you…' should be run together. This is achieved by deleting the carriage returns between the paragraphs.

Fionnuala marks the draft with the following symbols:

Dear wholesaler,

(A) We regret to inform you that, because of spiralling raw material costs, we have increased the price of some products. Our very popular Astrofoam has been increased from £11.75 to £12.50 per cubic metre. Our insulation foam for farm buildings, Agrifoam, has been increased from £8.50 to £9.20 per cubic metre. (B) The company has decided to extend its guarantee from ten to fifteen years on all of its insulation products. This fact should be made clear to the retailers, as our largest competitors only guarantee their products for seven years.

We are introducing a new insulation product called Bungafoam onto the market. This is suitable for bungalows, and is competitively priced at £11.50 per cubic metre.

(C) Our sales representative will be calling on you on 28 March. He will furnish you with all the dtails of our other insulation products and will accept your order this month.

I wish to remind you of our 5 per cent discount on all products that are paid for in full on the delivery date.

I am confident that you will continue to stock the Cavityfoam range of insulation products.

Yours faithfully,

Fionnuala O'Connor

Managing Director

A Move text to new position
B Start new paragraph
C Run on (not a new paragraph)

The letter will appear as follows after all these changes have been made:

Dear wholesaler,

We are introducing a new insulation product called Bungafoam onto the market. This is suitable for bungalows, and is competitively priced at £11.50 per cubic metre.

We regret to inform you that, because of spiralling raw material costs, we have increased the price of some products. Our very popular Astrofoam has been increased from £11.75 to £12.50 per cubic metre. Our insulation foam for farm buildings, Agrifoam, has been increased from £8.50 to £9.20 per cubic metre.

The company has decided to extend its guarantee from ten to fifteen years on all of its insulation products. This fact should be made clear to the retailers, as our largest competitors only guarantee their products for seven years.

Our sales representative will be calling on you on 28 March. He will furnish you with all the details of our other insulation products and will accept your order this month. I wish to remind you of our 5 per cent discount on all products that are paid for in full on the delivery date.

I am confident that you will continue to stock the Cavityfoam range of insulation products.

Yours faithfully,

Fionnuala O'Connor
Managing Director

It is obvious that these changes could not have been carried out on an ordinary typewriter without retyping the whole document.

3. Enhancing the appearance of a document

Most word-processors offer the user a number of features to enhance the appearance of the text—although these should be used sparingly in business documents, especially by a beginner. They include:

- centring and underlining key words and phrases
- altering the line spacing
- setting new margins and rearranging text accordingly

Centring and underlining

Centring a line means moving it so that it is half way between the left and right margins, making it stand out more clearly. This is very commonly used for headings.

Underlining a section of text means that a continuous line will be printed under this area when the document is printed (although it may not appear in the display).

Some word-processors also allow selected words to be printed in **bold type**. On dot-matrix printers this is usually achieved by printing over the same letters two or more times. To enhance a piece of text using one of these features, the text is usually first marked, and then the command to centre, underline or change to bold must be given.

Most word-processors also have a feature called **justification**, where the shorter lines of a document are spread out towards the right margin to make all the lines the same length (as in this paragraph). In business documents this is rarely an improvement over ordinary ('flush left') alignment, and it is never appropriate for letters.

The default setting on most word-processors for justification is off (i.e. flush left alignment), and for line spacing is 1. These settings can be altered by using the correct commands before text is entered. It is also possible to alter justification and line spacing settings after the text has been entered: the text can then be realigned to the new settings.

Patrick has prepared a statement describing the company's plans for overseas expansion. He has centred the heading at the top of the document, and has also used bold type and underlining for key phrases:

Cavityfoam Enterprises Ltd has decided to open a <u>new plant at Reims in France for the production of building insulation materials</u>. The outlay is projected to be £7.8 million, and at first the plant will employ thirty-five people. The town council has given approval for the construction of the factory, and it is hoped that production at the new plant will start in eighteen months. This venture will allow Cavityfoam Enterprises to gain a foothold in the European market for insulation products.

Altering the line spacing

The amount of spacing between the lines can also be altered on your word-processor. Letters and statements for publication in newspapers often have 'double line spacing'—with approximately the depth of another line of type between each line—as printers prefer to receive text in this form.

Setting new margins

The managing director may wish to have the statement submitted to the local newspaper for publication in the next edition. Newspapers sometimes like text for publication to have lines only 30 characters long. Patrick can reset the margins on his word-processor to allow a maximum line length of 30 characters, as well as changing to double line spacing. Centring, underlining and other enhancements are not used.

The document would now appear as follows:

New project

Cavityfoam Enterprises Ltd has

decided to open a new plant at

Reims in France for the production

of building insulation materials. The

outlay is projected to be £7.8

million, and at first the plant will

employ thirty-five people. The town

council has given approval for the

construction of the factory, and it is

hoped that production at the new

plant will start in eighteen months.

This venture will allow Cavityfoam

Enterprises to gain a foothold in

the European market for insulation

products.

4. The 'find and replace' facility

Sometimes you may have used a word in the course of typing a document and then decide to replace it with another. A word-processor offers you a facility with which you can replace one word with another, at one place in the document or at every occurrence of that word in the document.

In the document above, Patrick has used the word 'plant' three times. He can easily replace it with the word 'factory' by using the 'find and replace' facility on his word-processor. The document would now appear as follows:

New project

Cavityfoam Enterprises Ltd has decided to open a new factory at Reims in France for the production of building insulation materials. The outlay is projected to be £7.8 million, and at first the factory will employ thirty-five people. The town council has given approval for the construction of the factory, and it is hoped that production at the new factory will start in eighteen months. This venture will allow Cavityfoam Enterprises to gain a foothold in the European market for insulation products.

The 'find and replace' facility also allows you to replace entire phrases with alternative phrases. The length of phrase permitted may be limited, however.

5. Setting tabs

Our keyboard has a 'tab' key (short for 'tabulation'). When this key is pressed the cursor will jump a number of spaces horizontally. This saves us the inconvenience of continually using the space bar to get to a certain position in the text.

There are a number of positions or 'tabs' already set at equal distances across the line. We can abandon these, however, and set our own tabs. This is an essential facility when we want to enter text in columns.

Tabs can be set quite easily on a word-processor. You can change the number of tabs and their positions, thus varying the widths of columns and the space between them.

Patrick has been asked to list the prices of Cavityfoam products for the last three years in columns. The document appears as follows:

Product	1989	1990	1991
Agrifoam	7.80	8.50	9.20
Astrofoam	10.50	11.75	12.50
Bungafoam	—	—	11.50
Chip carpet	4.99	5.50	5.50
Floor seal	3.60	4.20	4.20
Mason tiles	1.80	2.20	2.20
Shedfoam	7.20	7.20	7.20

Patrick realises that the columns are too close together. He resets the tabs to adjust the distances between the columns. The document would now appear as follows:

Product	1989	1990	1991
Agrifoam	7.80	8.50	9.20
Astrofoam	10.50	11.75	12.50
Bungafoam	—	—	11.50
Chip carpet	4.90	5.50	5.50
Floor seal	3.60	4.20	4.20
Mason tiles	1.80	2.20	2.20
Shedfoam	7.20	7.20	7.20

6. Stored paragraphs

One of the most useful features of a word-processor is the ability to store frequently used paragraphs in separate files on disk. When we are entering text into a file on our word-processor we can copy one of the stored paragraphs into the file as required.

Many letters and documents produced on word-processors are the result of 'pasting together' a number of stored paragraphs (sometimes called 'boilerplate paragraphs').

Cavityfoam Enterprises Ltd interviewed five suitably qualified people for two positions in the quality control department. The interview board has made its selection and has asked Patrick to send letters to the applicants, telling them of the board's decision. Patrick will store the following paragraphs in separate files on disk:

[Paragraph 1]
We should like to thank you for attending for interview on Thursday last. We were very impressed by your qualifications and experience.

[Paragraph 2]
We wish to offer you the position of quality control assistant. Please confirm your acceptance of the position as soon as possible so that we can organise a suitable date for a medical examination. We look forward to hearing from you.

[Paragraph 3]
We are, however, unable to offer you a position with our company at the present time. We wish you every success in your future career.

[Paragraph 4]
Yours faithfully,

Fionnuala O'Connor
Managing Director

Patrick can open individual documents on his word-processor and use these paragraphs to compose appropriate letters.

Two of the applicants for jobs were Anne Breen and John Cuddy. Anne's efforts have been successful; John, however, has been unsuccessful. Both applicants will receive appropriate letters. The texts of these letters are as follows:

Letter 1: comprising stored paragraphs 1, 2, and 4

18 June 1991

Ms Anne Breen
4 Oakwood Road
Castlebawn, Co. Donegal

Dear Ms Breen

We should like to thank you for attending for interview on Thursday last. We were very impressed by your qualifications and experience.

We wish to offer you the position of quality control assistant. Please confirm your acceptance of the position as soon as possible so that we can organise a suitable date for a medical examination. We look forward to hearing from you.

Yours faithfully,

Fionnuala O'Connor
Managing Director

Letter 2: comprising stored paragraphs 1, 3, and 4

18 June 1991

Mr John Cuddy
31 Eskermore Terrace
Castlebawn, Co. Donegal

Dear Mr Cuddy

We should like to thank you for attending for interview on Thursday last. We were very impressed by your qualifications and experience.

We are, however, unable to offer you a position with our company at the present time. We wish you every success in your future career.

Yours faithfully,

Fionnuala O'Connor
Managing Director

The other three applicants would receive replies identical to one or other of the above letters.

This method of composing letters and documents from a set of stored paragraphs is widely used by people who use word-processors as a central part of their work. A lawyer's secretary may store on disk a range of paragraphs relating to contracts and other legal documents. Different sets of paragraphs can then be combined in a document, depending on the nature of the contract being drawn up.

7. Merge printing

One of the most powerful features of a word-processor is the merge printing facility. This allows you to draw up a **source file**, which usually consists of a single document or letter containing **variables**. The precise information to be included instead of the variables is entered in a **data file.** When you invoke merge printing, the various sets of data from the data file are merged into copies of the source file.

The managing director of Cavityfoam Enterprises Ltd has asked Patrick to send letters to wholesalers in three regions—south-west, south-east, and central—informing them of a demonstration of the new insulation product, Bungafoam. The details of the demonstration in each region are as follows:

Region	Time	Date	Venue
South-west	2 p.m.	3 April	Whiterock Hotel
South-east	3 p.m.	5 April	Silver Swan Hotel
Central	2 p.m.	10 April	Kilmore Hotel

Patrick would enter a source file in his word-processor like the one shown below:

19 March 1991

Dear wholesaler,

You are invited to a demonstration of our new insulation product for bungalows, called Bungafoam, at &time& on &date& in the &hotel&. This demonstration is for the benefit of all wholesalers in the &area& region.

There will be time after the demonstration for a discussion on the product. Any opinions or criticisms of the product will be welcome.

We look forward to seeing you at the demonstration.

Yours sincerely

Fionnuala O'Connor
Managing Director

Patrick would then set up a data file and include the times, dates, hotels and regions in a manner similar to that outlined below:

2 p.m.,3 April,Whiterock Hotel,south-west
3 p.m.,5 April,Silver Swan Hotel,south-east
2 p.m,10 April,Kilmore Hotel,central

You should check the exact format on your particular word-processor for variables in the source file and for data in the data file.

When Patrick invokes the merge printing facility, the details from the data file will be merged with the source file, and three separate documents will be produced for the three regions. The three letters should appear as follows:

Letter 1: South-west region

19 March 1991

Dear wholesaler,

You are invited to a demonstration of our new insulation product for bungalows, called Bungafoam, at 2 p.m. on 3 April in the Whiterock Hotel. This demonstration is for the benefit of all wholesalers in the south-west region.

There will be time after the demonstration for a discussion on the product. Any opinions or criticisms of the product will be welcome.

We look forward to seeing you at the demonstration.

Yours sincerely

Fionnuala O'Connor
Managing Director

Letter 2: South-east region

19 March 1991

Dear wholesaler,

You are invited to a demonstration of our new insulation product for bungalows, called Bungafoam, at 3 p.m. on 5 April in the Silver Swan Hotel. This demonstration is for the benefit of all wholesalers in the south-east region.

There will be time after the demonstration for a discussion on the product. Any opinions or criticisms of the product will be welcome.

We look forward to seeing you at the demonstration.

Yours sincerely

Fionnuala O'Connor
Managing Director

Letter 3: Central region

19 March 1991

Dear wholesaler,

You are invited to a demonstration of our new insulation product for bungalows, called Bungafoam, at 2 p.m. on 10 April in the Kilmore Hotel. This demonstration is for the benefit of all wholesalers in the central region.

There will be time after the demonstration for a discussion on the product. Any opinions or criticisms of the product will be welcome.

We look forward to seeing you at the demonstration.

Yours sincerely

Fionnuala O'Connor
Managing Director

Conclusion

We have examined some of the most frequently used facilities of word-processor programs. You can gain practice in using these facilities by attempting the assignments in the following chapter.

Chapter

9

Practical word-processing assignments

These assignments are graded, and we advise that you work through them in the order in which they are given. Unless otherwise stated, set the left margin to 1 and the right margin to 65 characters for all assignments. Justification should be off.

Functions and commands required

As you progress through these assignments you will need to check on the functions and commands specific to your word-processor program. You will also be practising commands and functions learned in earlier assignments. (*Note:* If you have not got access to a printer, you can display the results of that task instead).

The functions and commands required for each assignment are as follows:

ASSIGNMENT 1
- Text entry in a document file
- Cursor movement
- Saving a document to disk

ASSIGNMENT 2
- Deleting and inserting text

ASSIGNMENT 3
Consolidation assignment

ASSIGNMENT 4
- Moving a block of text

ASSIGNMENT 5
- Dividing and joining paragraphs

ASSIGNMENT 6
Consolidation assignment

ASSIGNMENT 7
- Centring

ASSIGNMENT 8
- Underlining and bold

ASSIGNMENT 1

You are required to enter the text below in your word-processor. When you have finished you should save the work onto disk in a file called LOCHHUNT and exit the system.

Nessie lies low

A prize of £1,500 in the Loch Ness monster hunt was won yesterday by Oceanscan, an American survey company. The prize, however, fell far short of the £250,000 on offer for conclusive proof of Nessie's existence.

Oceanscan made sonar contact on Saturday with a large unidentified object measuring up to 8 m long. The sonar contact was made near the loch's northern shore, where most sightings of Nessie have been reported.

Andy James (42), the team leader, said yesterday: 'We are thrilled to win the prize for the best search method. The object, which showed up on Saturday, registered as two blips on the sonar screen, but it moved out of range quickly.'

The organising committee of the hunt have decided to hold the event again next year. It will be held over a ten-day period in July, and the prize money for conclusive proof of Nessie's existence will be increased to £300,000. Many teams, including those from Canada and the United States, have agreed to participate again.

Carry out the following tasks:

Recall LOCHHUNT to the screen and practise the various cursor movement commands for your word-processor.

ASSIGNMENT 2

You are required to enter the news extract below in your word-processor and save it on disk, using OILFIND1 as the file name and exit the system.

New oil reserves

Saudi Arabia has discovered extensive new crude oil reserves in previously unexplored areas, according to a report from Reuters news agency today.

One Saudi government source said that the new find was bigger than the total known reserves of some other OPEC member-states. The Saudi state company has reportedly been drilling in areas well away from its existing oil pipeline network.

The agency quotes unnamed Saudi officials as saying that the find could boost the country's oil reserves by as much as 20 per cent. The discovery could have a significant impact on oil markets, in lowering the price of crude oil from its recent record price of around $40 per barrel.

This is good news for the consumer, who has recently been experiencing steadily increasing prices on all oil products. Increased oil prices automatically lead to increased inflation and invariably to increases in unemployment.

Carry out the following tasks:

[1] Recall OILFIND1 to the screen.

[2] Edit the file by making the alterations shown below.

New oil reserves

Saudi Arabia has discovered extensive new crude oil reserves in previously unexplored areas, according to a report from Reuters news agency ~~today~~ *yesterday*

One Saudi government source said that the new find was bigger than the total known reserves of some other OPEC member-states. The Saudi state *oil* company has reportedly been drilling in areas well away from its existing oil pipeline network.

The agency quotes unnamed Saudi officials as saying that the ~~find~~ *discovery* could boost the country's oil reserves by as much as 20 per cent. The discovery could have a significant impact on *world* oil markets, in lowering the price of crude oil from its recent record price of around $40 per barrel.

This is good news for the consumer, who has recently been experiencing steadily increasing prices on all oil products. Increased oil prices ~~automatically~~ lead to increased inflation and invariably to increases in unemployment.

---

[3] Save this edited version of the file onto your disk, using OILFIND2 as the file name.

[4] Print OILFIND1 and OILFIND2.

ASSIGNMENT 3

Following the inaugural meeting of Dunbeg Residents' Association, a set of proposals was drawn up for the attention of the county council. The proposals are outlined in the document below. You are required to enter this document in your word-processor and save it onto your disk, using DUNBEG1 as the file name.

Dunbeg development proposals

There is an immediate need for a children's playground in the area. The association considers Knockmore Meadow as a suitable site for a playground, as it is close to Dunbeg swimming pool and gymnasium. The association is prepared to organise and supervise sports events and barbecues during the summer holidays.

There is an immediate need for a pedestrian crossing on Castledean Road near the shopping arcade. Residents of Beechwood Road and Fitzgerald Avenue have great difficulty crossing Castledean Road during working hours.

The association urges the county council to honour its 1988 commitment to install street lights on Bishopstown Road and Gasfinn Road. These roads are close to the railway station, and the lack of adequate street lighting, especially during winter months, is a problem for those who commute to Castledean every day.

Carry out the following tasks:

[1] Recall DUNBEG1 to the screen.

[2] Edit the document by making the alterations shown below.

Dunbeg development proposals

There is an ~~immediate~~ _urgent_ need for a children's playground in the area. The association considers Knockmore Meadow ~~as~~ _to be_ a suitable site for a playground, as it is close to Dunbeg swimming pool and gymnasium. The association is prepared to organise and supervise sports events and barbecues ~~during~~ _at the playground_ the summer holidays.

There is an immediate need for a pedestrian crossing on Castledean Road near the shopping ~~arcade~~ _centre_. Residents of Beechwood Road and Fitzgerald Avenue have great difficulty crossing Castledean Road during working hours.

The association urges the county council to honour its 198~~8~~_9_ commitment to install street light_ing_ on Bishopstown Road and Glasfinn Road. These roads are close to the railway station, and the lack of adequate street lighting, especially during winter months, is a problem for those who commute _by rail_ to Castledean every day.

[3] Save the edited version of the file to disk, using DUNBEG2 as the file name.

[4] Print DUNBEG1 and DUNBEG2.

ASSIGNMENT 4

You are required to enter the document below in your word-processor. You should then save the document onto your disk, using NEWS as the file name.

Mason & Co.

COMPANY NEWSLETTER

INTERCOMPANY FOOTBALL. The annual intercompany football tournament took place at Murrenstown football grounds. Many local firms entered a team. The tournament was eventually won by Slaney Meats PLC. Our team reached the semi-final but was beaten by Marymount Electrical Ltd.

FISHING TRIP. Twenty-five people have enlisted for the fishing trip to the Slane valley on Saturday next. A coach will leave from the town hall at 10 a.m. A limited number of places is still available; if you are interested, please forward your name to John Martin or Susan Conway.

NEW ARRIVAL. Best wishes to Andrew and Niamh Boylan on the birth of their first child, a baby girl. She is to be called Ciara.

DRAMA SECTION. Mary McEvoy would like to hear from anyone who would be willing to participate in this year's drama production of John B. Keane's 'Many Young Men of Twenty'. Performances would be in late March of next year.

SECURE PARKING. In the light of last month's vandalism of two cars in the company car park, a new gate has been installed at the entrance to the car park. This gate will be locked from 10 a.m. to 1 p.m. and from 2:15 to 4:45 p.m. each day.

Carry out the following tasks:

[1] Produce a print-out of NEWS (or use the text above).

[2] Recall NEWS to the screen and make the alterations shown below.

Mason & Co.

COMPANY NEWSLETTER

Position here →

INTERCOMPANY FOOTBALL. The annual intercompany football tournament took place at Murrenstown ~~football~~ *sports* grounds. Many local firms entered a team. The tournament was eventually won by Slaney Meat PLC. Our team reached the semi-final but was beaten *in a penalty shootout* by Marymount Electrical Ltd.

FISHING TRIP. Twenty-five people have enlisted for the fishing trip to the ~~Slane~~ *Boyne* valley on Saturday next. A coach will leave from the town hall at 10 a.m. A limited number of places is still available; if you are interested, please forward your name *and address* to John Martin or Susan Conway.

NEW ARRIVAL. Best wishes to Andrew and Niamh Boylan on the birth of their first child, a baby girl. She is to be called Ciara.

DRAMA SECTION. Mary McEvoy would like to hear from anyone who would be willing to participate in this year's drama production of John B. Keane's 'Many Young Men of Twenty'. Performances would be in ~~late March~~ *early April* of next year.

SECURE PARKING. In the light of last month's vandalism of two cars in the company car park, a new gate has been installed at the entrance to the car park. This gate will be locked from 10 a.m. to 1 p.m. and from 2:15 to 4:45 p.m. each day.

Take back to previous page. Position where shown by asterix. ✻

[3] Save the edited version of the file to your disk, using NEWS1 as the file name.

[4] Produce a print-out of NEWS1.

ASSIGNMENT 5

You are required to enter the following letter in your word-processor and save it to disk, using CARSALE1 as the file name.

Cox Motors Ltd
Gort Road
Ballymore, Co. Tipperary

Our ref.: TD/AR

11 May 1991

Mr Ruairí O'Connell
25 Golden Vale Road
Ballymore, Co. Tipperary

Dear Mr O'Connell,

Thank you for your enquiry about the Astra car range.

As requested, we are sending you a brochure giving full details of all six cars in the range.

You will notice that the fuel consumption is excellent and that all models can use unleaded petrol. It is also worth noting that each new Astra has a three-year warranty on all parts. All Astras are equipped with stereo radio and compact disc player, central locking, and rear window wipers. A sun-roof and metallic paint are optional extras.

A leaflet is also enclosed outlining the retail prices of our new cars, together with a comprehensive list of prices of quality used Astra cars in stock.

Please feel free to drop into the garage at any time for a test drive in an Astra.

Yours faithfully,

Desmond Cox
Sales Department

Carry out the following tasks:

[1] Produce a print-out of the file (or use the text on the previous page).

[2] Edit the letter by marking it with the symbols you have learnt, making the following changes:

(*a*) replace the date given above with today's date;

(*b*) in paragraph 2, replace 'car' with 'model';

(*c*) delete the word 'also' in paragraph 3;

(*d*) insert the word 'now' before 'in stock' at the end of paragraph 4;

(*e*) replace 'drop' with 'call' in paragraph 5;

(*f*) join the first two paragraphs together;

(*g*) make the sentence that begins 'All Astras are equipped...' the start of a new paragraph.

[3] Recall CARSALE1 to the screen and make these alterations to the file.

[4] Save this version of the letter to your disk, using CARSALE2 as the file name.

[5] Produce a print-out of CARSALE2.

ASSIGNMENT 6

You are required to enter the following document in your word-processor and save it to disk, using AGM1 as the file name:

Minutes of the annual general meeting of members of Corrugated Steel Products Ltd, held at 34 Riverside Road, Navan, on Tuesday 30 October 1990.

Mr Aidan Dooley, Chairman of the Board, presided.

1. The Secretary read the notice convening the meeting, and the auditors' report.

2. The Chairman addressed the meeting, and proposed: That the directors' report and the accounts for the year ending 30 September 1990 produced at the meeting be hereby received and adopted, and that a dividend of 15 per cent less income tax be declared, to be payable to members on 20 November 1990.

3. The Chairman proposed that Mr Patrick Matthews, the director retiring by rotation, be re-elected as a director of the company. Mr Declan Murphy seconded the motion, which was put to the meeting and carried unanimously.

4. Ms Niamh Sheridan, a shareholder, proposed that Jackson, Brady and Company, having agreed to continue in office as auditors for a further year, receive a fixed fee of £17,000. This was seconded by Mr Seán Moran, another shareholder, put to the meeting, and carried unanimously.

5. There was no other business.

Chairman

7 November 1990

Carry out the following tasks:

[1] Produce a print-out of AGM1 (or use the text above).

[2] Edit the minutes by marking the print-out with the symbols you have learnt, making the following changes:

      (*a*) the correct name of the company is Corrugated Iron Products Ltd;

      (*b*) the dividend declared was 18 per cent, not 15 per cent;

      (*c*) the dividend will be paid to members one week later than the date given above;

      (*d*) the motion to re-elect Patrick Matthews was not carried unanimously but by nine votes to two;

      (*e*) change the order of items 3 and 4 as they appear in the document (remember to change the numbers).

[3] Recall AGM1 to the screen and make these alterations to the file.

[4] Save the altered document to disk, using AGM2 as the file name.

[5] Produce a print-out of AGM2.

ASSIGNMENT 7

You are required to type in the following menu for the Ideal Hotel. Call this file MENU.

IDEAL HOTEL
14 Rose Garden Mews
Rathgannon, Co. Cork

MENU

Mandarin & grapefruit cocktail
or
Chicken and mushroom vol-au-vent
***
Prime cut of roast beef with horseradish sauce
or
Loin of pork rolled with savoury stuffing & cucumber
or
Roast turkey with onion and sage stuffing and baked Limerick ham
or
Prime sirloin of steak bordelaise
or
Poached Moy salmon hollandaise
***
Selection of fresh seasonal vegetables
***
Baked alaska
or
Peach Melba & ice cream
or
Home-made apple tart and fresh cream
or
Sherry trifle chantilly
***
Tea or coffee
After-dinner mints
£14.75 per person

Carry out the following tasks:

[1] The menu is to be displayed outside the hotel, but the manager is not pleased with the format. He has asked you to centre all the text, including the hotel name and address. Recall the file MENU and make this change.

[2] Save the centred menu to disk, using MENUC as the file name.

[3] Produce a print-out of MENUC.

ASSIGNMENT 8

You are required to type in the following report on the decline of sales in the south of the country, and save it as REPORT.

REPORT OF THE SUBCOMMITTEE

This is the report of the subcommittee appointed according to the terms of the Board resolution of 5 July 1990 'that a subcommittee be appointed to investigate and report on the decline of sales in the southern region for the period ending 30 November 1990, and to make recommendations.'

Subcommittee members
   Frank Brady (chairman)
   Valerie Byrne
   Ian Caprani
   Ciarán Dunne
   Madeleine Dunne
   Dermot Moyne
   Mary Purcell

Summary
The full report is in the hands of the marketing manager. Some of the more important findings are:

   (*a*) Competition has increased considerably, especially with the entry into the market of Reprotext Ltd.

   (*b*) Two of our reliable customers have ceased trading in the last twelve months: Southprint Ltd and Speedprint Ltd.

   (*c*) There is a cheaper imported paper on the market, which is affecting sales from department C.

   (*d*) Because of the high rate of absenteeism in the dispatch department some orders were cancelled.

   (*e*) The haulier for the southern region is less reliable than those of any of the other regions.

Recommendations
   1. Find a new haulier for the southern region.

   2. Obtain more information on possible cheaper sources of paper.

   3. Assign two more sales representatives to the region.

   4. Establish the reason for the absenteeism in the dispatch department.

   5. Make a closer examination of the activities of Reprotext Ltd.

Data
Details of data relevant to this report are attached.

Signed: ....

1 December 1990

Carry out the following tasks:

[1] Recall this document and make the following changes to make the report more attractive-looking:

(a) underline all subheadings in the document;

(b) change the heading of the report to bold, and centre it.

(c) change any company name in the document to bold.

[2] Save the document as REPORTA.

ASSIGNMENT

You are required to type in the following letter, which was sent to the *Irish Daily* by a reader. Save the document as OUTDOOR.

91 St Peter's Drive
Dublin 24

5 July 1991

Dear sir,

I am writing to describe a recent experience that might be of interest to your readers.

I decided to do something different for my holidays this year. I booked an adventure holiday at the Slievemore Mountain Lodge adventure centre in Co. Wicklow. From the very minute I arrived at the centre I began to unwind. The scenery was beautiful, with peaceful lakes, rolling heather-covered hills, and sparkling streams.

The centre has a choice of daily activities, including hill walking, canoeing, sailing, orienteering, and rock climbing, to mention only a few. I tried nearly all of these activities during the week. The walks covered an area where we saw no signs of human habitation, which made a pleasant contrast with the 'concrete jungle' I am used to most of the year! The accommodation was very comfortable: it was a real pleasure to return from a day's activity to a roaring log fire and a hot meal.

We hear so much about disappointed holidaymakers nowadays. This was the best holiday of my life, and I would wholeheartedly recommend such a holiday to anyone who wants a real break from it all.

Yours sincerely,

Pádraig Whelan

Carry out the following tasks:

[1] To make it more acceptable to the editor of the paper, the letter should be put into a narrow column. Recall the file OUTDOOR and change the margin settings to: left, 10 characters; right, 40 characters (30 characters wide), and realign the text within the new margins.

[2] Save the letter as OUTDOOR 1.

ASSIGNMENT 10

You are required to enter the following text into your word-processor and save it to disk, using SURVEY as the file name.

HEART DISEASE SURVEY

More than half of a group of patients screened for heart disease risk factors were found to be overweight, and nearly a quarter had high blood pressure, it emerged today.

The researchers looked at forty patients in the Dún Laoghaire area. GPs screened the patients for such things as excess weight, high blood pressure, and high cholesterol levels.

Now researchers are planning a second screening project, to study a larger number of patients, following the disturbing results of the pilot study carried out by the Department of Preventive Medicine in University College, Dublin.

Nearly 60 per cent of the people examined were overweight, according to the 'Irish Medical Times'. A quarter had high cholesterol levels, while 20 to 30 per cent had high blood pressure.

Now, GPs in the wider area of south-east Co. Dublin are to become involved in a second trial to screen a larger number of patients.

Carry out the following tasks:

[1] Produce a print-out of SURVEY (or use the text above).

[2] Edit the print-out, using the symbols you have already learnt, to make the following alterations to the text:

(*a*) change the heading to bold;

(*b*) in paragraph 1, 'nearly a quarter' should read 'nearly a third';

(*c*) in paragraph 2, 'researchers looked at forty patients' should read 'researchers examined medical reports on forty patients';

(*d*) in paragraph 2 also, change 'Dún Laoghaire area' to bold;

(*e*) in paragraph 3, 'researchers are planning' should read 'researchers are already planning';

(*f*) in paragraph 3 also, underline 'Department of Preventive Medicine';

(*g*) in paragraph 5, 'south-east Co. Dublin' should read 'south Co. Dublin';

(*h*) change the order of paragraphs 2 and 3.

[3] Recall SURVEY to the screen and make these changes to the file.

[4] Alter the margins to 5 and 60, and realign the text within the new margins.

[5] Save the edited version of the file to your disk, using SURVEY2 as the file name.

[6] Produce a print-out of SURVEY2.

You are required to type in the following letter informing a customer of a new product. Save the letter as NEWPROD.

MOUNTAINGEAR LTD
Glenview, Co. Kildare
Telephone (048) 52345

19 April 1991

The Outdoor Shop
62 Fleet Street
Dublin 2

Dear sir,

We are writing to inform you of a new product in our range, the Eiger storm tent.

The shape of the Eiger has been designed to give top performance in fierce weather. Tensions have been carefully worked out so that all strains are equally distributed over the whole surface. The tunnel shape, formed by two supporting hoops, is chosen because of its aerodynamic efficiency and because it offers more usable volume inside than all other tent shapes. Further stability is created by the canting of the two poles at an angle. This improves Eiger performance under a snow load.

The interior space of Eiger is remarkable for a relatively small tent. This allows for greater comfort when using the Eiger for long periods in extreme weather. The front bell end has plenty of working space and has two zips, giving a choice of entry.

Ease of setting up the tent was another important consideration in developing Eiger. The tent can be erected in less than two minutes by one person, even in strong wind.

Enclosed is a detailed specification and photograph of the Eiger. A display tent can be delivered if requested.

Yours faithfully,

Liam Burns
Sales Manager

Carry out the following tasks:

[1] Before sending these letters to different customers, the marketing manager decided to change the name of the product: the new name is Everest. Use the 'find and replace' facility (if available) to make this change anywhere the name Eiger is mentioned in the letter.

[2] Save this version of the letter as NEWPROD1.

ASSIGNMENT 12

You are required to type in the following daily timetable for an introductory computer course. You should use tabs to help in the aligning of the text; tab settings should be as follows:

First tab: 18
Second tab: 42
Third tab: 59

Course: Introduction to computing			
Time	Details	Tutor	Room
9:30	Introduction to computer hardware	Ms M. Purcell	Com1
10:30	Coffee break		
10:50	Introduction to computer software	Dr D. Cox	Com1
11:30	Keyboarding	Ms G. Coakley	Com2
12:30	Lunch		
1:30	Hands-on word-processing	Prof. J. O'Brien	Com2
2:30	Hands-on spreadsheets	Dr A. Clifford	Com2
3:30	Coffee		
3:50	Hands-on data-base	Dr D. Cooney	Com2
4:30	Networking; electronic mail; computer safety	Mr M. Keenan	Com2
5:30	Review		

Save the document as TABS, and print it.

ASSIGNMENT 13

You have just been appointed to the complaints department of Hewson Electrical Ltd. Your duties include responding to letters of complaint from dissatisfied customers.

You are required to save each of the following paragraphs in separate files on your disk. The files should be named PT1, PT2, PT3, PT4, and PT5, respectively.

[File 1]
We have received your letter concerning the item that you bought at our store. We are sorry to hear that it is causing problems.

[File 2]
As the goods are still under guarantee, please call our maintenance department to arrange a suitable time for our repair technician to call to you.

[File 3]
As the goods are no longer under guarantee, repair work cannot be carried out free of charge. Our repair technician, however, can call to you to give a quotation for the cost of repairs.

[File 4]
As this is an old model, parts are extremely difficult to obtain. We have an excellent range of new models in our showrooms, and we would be happy to offer you a reasonable trade-in discount off the cost of a new model.

[File 5]
Yours faithfully,

Desmond Joyce
Repair Control Department

Carry out the following tasks:

Use the correct combination of stored paragraphs and today's date to compose letters of reply to the following customers. You are also given suitable names for your letter files.

Letter	Person	Stored paragraphs
LTR1	Ms Joyce Noonan 55 Kilmore Road Castlebawn, Co. Donegal	Files: PT1, PT2, PT5
LTR2	Mr Seán Ryan 73 Ormond Road Invermore, Co. Limerick	Files: PT1, PT3, PT5
LTR3	Ms Róisín Nestor 6 Mount Nugent Road Dunfinn, Co. Cavan	Files: PT1, PT4, PT5

ASSIGNMENT 14

As personnel manager of Green Valley Foods Ltd you must recruit a new secretary for the managing director of the company. You have advertised the position in the local press and have received a large number of applications.

You have decided to call three suitably qualified people for interview, and to use the merge printing facility of your word-processor to compose letters to these three people requesting them to attend for interview.

The standard letter is as follows:

&person&
&address1&
&address2&
17 May 1991

Dear &name&,

We are pleased to invite you to an interview for the post of secretary to the managing director of our company, on &date& at &time&.

You should call at the reception desk in the front hall. The receptionist will direct you to &location&.

Please confirm that you will be able to attend at that time.

Yours faithfully,

Mary Thompson
Personnel Manager

Carry out the following tasks:

[1] Enter the text of the letter as given above. Here the ampersand (&) is used to enclose the variables: different indicators may be required on your word-processor. Save the letter in a file called NEWJOB.

[2] Create a data file called PEOPLE, using the data given below.

person:	Ms Aisling Downey	Mr Paul Ryan	Ms Patricia Burke
address1:	3 Willowbrook Road	45 Collins Park	12 Rosslee Road
address2:	Kilpatrick, Co. Cork	Kilpatrick, Co. Cork	Kilpatrick, Co. Cork
name:	Ms Downey	Mr Ryan	Ms Burke
date:	26 May 1991	26 May 1991	26 May 1991
time:	10:30 a.m.	2:15 p.m.	3:30 p.m.
location:	room 19	room 22	room 22

[3] Use the merge printing facility on your word-processor to merge the data from the file PEOPLE with the standard letter in the file NEWJOB.

You are required to type in the following document, which is a report on the valuation and condition of a property that a client is thinking of buying. The appropriate tab settings should also be used in typing the columns in the 'Accommodation' section.

SHOWPIECE AUCTIONEERS
3 Ringsend Green
Dublin 4

VALUATION REPORT

Property: 76 Mountain Road
               Dublin 16

Clients: Mr Peter Flanagan and Ms Mary Flanagan
               8 Terenure Drive
               Dublin 6

In accordance with your instructions we inspected the above property to ascertain the current market value and condition. Our report follows.

Location
The property is situated within a modern residential development beside St Peter's Park and all other amenities. It is approximately 4 km from Rathgar centre and approximately 10 km south of Dublin city centre.

Description
The gross internal floor area is approximately 114 square metres. The property comprises a two-storey mainly block-built semi-detached house with maple timber floors. Windows throughout are double-glazed in all rooms. The roof is concrete-tiled and pitched. The house has a half-brick front elevation, otherwise Tyrolean front, rear and side elevations.

Accommodation
Glazed entrance porch.
Spacious hallway with telephone.
Sitting-room: 4.5 X 4.2 m, with inset fireplace. Double doors to:
Dining-room: 3.75 X 4.5 m, with patio doors.
Kitchen: 3.75 X 3.5 m, with stainless sink unit and oak fitted presses.
   Upstairs there are three bedrooms:
Bedroom 1: 4.25 X 4 m, with double built-in wardrobes, and bathroom with shower en suite.
Bedroom 2: 2.75 X 4.25 m, with built-in wardrobe.
Bedroom 3: 2.75 X 2.75 m, with fitted shelving.
Bathroom: with three-piece suite.
Hot press with dual immersion heater.

Outside
Mature landscaped gardens to front and rear; garage with fuse-box and gas meter.

Services
All main services are available, including gas-fired central heating.

Title
Freehold.

Condition of the property
In our surveyor's report it is noted that the property is in excellent structural order, but some attention should be given to the maintenance of the fascia and soffit sheeting at the rear of the property. A small crack at the gable wall under the window-sill needs to be repaired immediately.

Valuation
In our opinion the present market value of the property, subject to the foregoing work being carried out, is in the region of   £62,000.00
(sixty-two thousand pounds)

Signed: ....

Date: ....

Carry out the following tasks:

[1] Save the report as VALUE, and print it (or use the text on the previous page).

[2] Edit the print-out, using the symbols you have already learnt, to make the following alterations to the text:

(*a*) change the headings 'Property' and 'Clients' to bold;

(*b*) centre and underline the subheadings 'Location' to 'Valuation';

(*c*) in the section headed 'Location' delete the word 'modern', and change 'Rathgar' to 'Rathmines';

(*d*) in the section headed 'Description' change 'maple' to 'pine' and delete the words 'in all rooms'; move the first sentence of this paragraph so that it becomes the last sentence;

(*e*) change the names of the rooms in the 'Accommodation' section, from 'Sitting-room' to 'Bathroom', to bold;

(*f*) in the section headed 'Condition of the property' insert 'wooden' before 'fascia'; make the last sentence the beginning of a new paragraph.

[3] Recall VALUE to the screen and make these changes to the file.

[4] Save the report as VALUE1, and print it.

Chapter 10

Word-processing concepts

The following topics will be discussed in this chapter:

1. Types of word-processor
2. Basic word-processor facilities
3. Other facilities
4. Layout and presentation
5. The word-processor display
6. Paper
7. Document output
8. Applications
9. Advantages of word-processor use
10. Disadvantages of word-processor use

1. Types of word-processor

When we speak of using a word-processor we usually mean a microcomputer running a word-processor program. However, it is also possible to buy a special-purpose or 'dedicated' word-processor: one that is specifically designed to perform word-processing tasks only. This is also a microcomputer, but its CPU is specially designed to manipulate text: it cannot be used to perform any other tasks. The word-processor program is usually contained in the ROM of the computer and programmed at the time of manufacture.

Many businesses installed special-purpose word-processors as replacements for typewriters when the staff of these businesses were still unfamiliar with—or indeed nervous of—computers, or could not imagine what other uses they would have in an office.

Popular microcomputers are now so powerful that they can carry out any word-processing task rapidly and effectively; and with a general-purpose computer it is possible to choose whichever of the many widely available word-processor programs you prefer.

The microcomputer is designed to run a variety of programs. A particular program needs only to be loaded into the RAM of the microcomputer from a disk so that it can be used. When finished using the word-processor you can load a different type of program, for example an accounts program. The ability of microcomputers to run a variety of programs makes them versatile tools, whereas the special-purpose word-processor can only be used for one purpose.

2. Basic word-processor facilities

Word wraparound

When you enter text with a word-processor it appears on the display in front of you as you type. When the end of a line (wherever you have set your right margin) is reached, the cursor moves automatically to the beginning of the next line.

Carriage return

When you run a word-processor program on your computer the 'enter' key becomes the 'carriage return' key. Pressing this key causes the current line to end wherever you happen to be, and the cursor moves to the beginning of the next line, thus creating a new paragraph. A carriage return is sometimes called a 'hard carriage return', to distinguish it from the temporary or 'soft' carriage return produced by word wraparound.

Page break

You can make the text start printing on a new page by entering a command that causes a page break. This is a code entered into the file that causes the printer to act as if the end of a page has been reached. With single-sheet printing the printer will eject the current page when the page break code is encountered and then stop, and will continue when a new sheet is fed in; with fan-fold stationery the paper will move up and printing will continue on a new page.

The page break code is sometimes called a 'forced page break', to distinguish it from the kind that occurs automatically when the amount of text you have typed would fill a page. Both kinds of page break cause a special mark to appear on the display to show you that you are at the beginning of a new page.

Editing

Many other facilities for moving or changing text are available with most word-processors, either when typing text in or after typing. They include the following:

- inserting characters, words, lines, sentences, and paragraphs
- deleting characters, words, lines, sentences, and paragraphs
- moving and copying words, lines, sentences, and paragraphs
- automatic realignment of the text after inserting, deleting, moving, or copying
- changing left and right margins
- setting and changing tabs
- setting and changing line spacing
- justification
- centring, underlining, and bold type
- copying, combining and deleting files

Stored paragraphs

You can make up a composite document by combining any number of stored paragraphs containing different pieces of information. Sometimes information from other sources can be read into a word-processor document; for example, if you need to include information from a spreadsheet in a report, you might be able to read the spreadsheet into the text instead of retyping the information.

Text storage

Text that is keyed into a computer can be 'saved' or stored on your disk for later retrieval. This can be on either a fixed disk ('hard disk') or a diskette ('floppy disk').

It is this facility that gives word-processors one of their greatest advantages. On an electronic typewriter a one-line memory is available. This means that before printing a line on the paper you can change any part of that line. Once the 'enter' key is pressed the printed text cannot be retrieved or edited again. Stored text on a word-processor can be retrieved almost immediately from disk or at any later time.

Printing

When you have a printer linked to your word-processor your text can be printed on paper. This is of course the final objective of word-processing! High-quality printing can be achieved when a laser printer is used.

3. Other facilities

'Find and replace'

The use of the 'find and replace' feature has already been described. An interesting use of it was demonstrated recently when the author of a novel that was written on a word-processor decided in his wisdom to change the name of the main character. He used the 'find and replace' facility to change over four thousand references to the character's name before handing the new script to his editor. Could you imagine having to do this manually?

Spelling check

This is a most useful facility, available on fully featured word-processors. Every word in the document to be checked is compared against a list of words in one of the program files; any word not found is highlighted, and the computer may then give you a list of alternative spellings, or you can edit it yourself. If the word is correct but not in the word-processor's main list (for example place-names, personal names, or technical terms) then you usually have the facility to add it to the list, so that it will pass the test in the future.

Thesaurus

Many word-processors nowadays offer a thesaurus facility. This allows you to check individual words while entering or editing the document; for each word queried there is a list of alternative words with approximately the same meaning or a related meaning, and you may select any one of these and substitute it. Often the thesaurus will also give you a dictionary definition of the highlighted word.

Merge printing

This is a facility that allows you to set up a standard document file containing variables, and a data file containing the precise details that are to replace the variables. You can then merge the two files, producing customised multiple copies of the same document.

Merge printing is very useful in generating personalised letters from a standard letter, for example invitations to individual salespeople to a general meeting of sales staff at a company's head office.

4. Layout and presentation

The word-processor offers many features that allow us to enhance the layout and appearance of a document.

Change of typeface

Typefaces are distinctive styles of type, each with its own name. Some computer typefaces attempt to reproduce the appearance of traditional typefaces used in the printing of books; others may have been specially designed for your computer or printer. Typefaces come in special program files called **fonts**, usually with a separate font for each size of a particular typeface. The range of typefaces available to you will depend on your word-processor and also on the printer you are using.

Computer typefaces are grouped according to **pitch**, which refers to the number of characters that are printed per 25 mm (1 in.). Common typefaces are 10-pitch or 12-pitch, while 'condensed' or narrow typefaces may have a pitch of 15 or more. A different system is used with laser printers.

Change of alignment

The text of a document may be flush left, flush right, centred, or justified.

Text that is **flush left** has a straight left margin and lines of different length, exactly as it was typed into the word-processor. This is the normal style for letters and most business documents.

With **flush right** alignment we have the opposite of flush left: the lines are of different length, but it is the right margin that is straight and the left margin uneven. This style is rarely required except in advertisements, and many word-processors will not produce this alignment automatically.

As the name implies, **centred** text is adjusted so that it is half way between the left and right margins. Headings in books and documents are often centred.

In **justified** text both margins are straight: all the lines are forced out to equal length by increasing the space between words. This gives the text a squared-off appearance, which is the normal style for books and periodicals, but is usually not very successful with word-processor documents, except when a laser printer is available. Justification should not be used for letters.

Change of line spacing

As we have already seen, line spacing is the vertical distance between lines of text. The default setting is normally 1 or single line spacing. When you change this setting to 2 or double line spacing, a blank line will automatically be inserted between each line of text as you type; line spacing set at 3 will give the equivalent of two blank lines between each line of text.

5. The word-processor display

When you are typing text with your word-processor, the display will usually show some or all of the following:

Status line

This is a highlighted line across the top (e.g. Wordstar) or the bottom (e.g. Word, Wordperfect) of the display that tells you the current position of the cursor in the text: for example, P4 L9 C34 would tell you that the cursor is now at character 34 on line 9 of page 4. The status line usually also gives the name of the file you are working on and the disk it is on, and may also give you information about other features that are at present selected.

Menu

This is a list of options or commands now available. For example, you could consult the menu for the command for saving your document onto disk.

Ruler line

This line usually appears just above the work area. It defines the present position of the left and right margins and the position of any tabs you may have set.

Work area

This is the portion of the screen remaining for the display of your text. As you type it in, or recall it from disk, your text will appear in this area.

6. Paper

Paper types and sizes

Fan-fold paper is widely used with computer printers, as it feeds more reliably and more quickly; after printing it is usually separated into single sheets. For certain purposes, such as letters, individual sheets of paper may be preferable.

Nowadays most paper comes in one of the international standard sizes known as the 'A series', in which each size is exactly half of the next higher one, as shown in the diagram below.

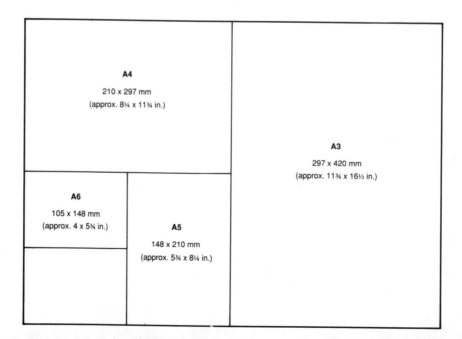

The number of lines that can be accommodated on a single page depends on the number of lines per vertical centimetre (this may be expressed in lines per inch on your computer) for which your word-processor is set. The following are the maximum numbers for A4 and A5 paper, with vertical ('portrait') and horizontal ('landscape') orientation:

Number of vertical lines possible					
lines/cm	(lines/in.)	Portrait		Landscape	
		A4	A5	A4	A5
4.75	12	140	99	99	70
4	10	117	82	82	58
3.25	8	94	66	66	47
2.25	6	70	49	49	35

The pitch, as we have seen, is the number of characters that can be accommodated per horizontal 25 mm (1 in.). The following table gives the maximum number of characters per line for different pitches:

Pitch	Maximum line length in characters			
	Portrait		Landscape	
	A4	A5	A4	A5
12	99	70	141	99
10	82	58	117	82
9	74	52	105	74
8	66	47	94	66

Paper quality

Paper is graded according to its relative weight, expressed in grams per square metre (g/m^2). Obviously, better-quality paper is heavier than poorer-quality paper. The most common grades of paper are:

$40 \ g/m^2$	'bank' or airmail paper
70 to $80 \ g/m^2$	standard paper
$90 \ g/m^2$	high-quality paper

7. Document output

Nowadays, many word-processors provide what is called a 'WYSIWYG' display (pronounced 'wizzywig'). This means that 'what you see [on the display] is what you get [on the print-out].'

You can obviously alter the layout of text to suit various paper sizes by changing margins and line spacing. You can change the pitch or typeface, and even override page length settings by entering forced page breaks.

The layout of the document as printed may be radically different from that originally entered into the word-processor.

Page volume calculation

We can calculate the number of characters that can be accommodated on a page, the margins to be set, and the number of lines on the page, provided we know the following:

(*a*) the paper size;
(*b*) the depth of the top and bottom margins (in number of lines);
(*c*) the width of the left and right margins;
(*d*) the pitch setting of the printer;
(*e*) the number of lines per vertical centimetre.

Let us take an example. Assuming that text is to printed in 10-pitch type on A4 paper (297 by 210 mm—11.75 by 8.25 in.), with a margin all round of 25 mm (1 in.), calculate the maximum number of characters per line and the number of lines that can be accommodated on a single page. Suggest suitable margin settings.

When we subtract our margin widths from the page size we find that the space available for printing purposes is 247 by 160 mm (9.75 by 6.25 in.). It is conventional to assume for 10-pitch printing that 6 lines are accommodated per vertical 25 mm (1 in.); the number of lines that can be accommodated satisfactorily on our page therefore is the depth (247) divided by 25 and multiplied by 6, or 59, giving 59 lines.

The number of 10-pitch characters that can be accommodated satisfactorily on one line is 160 divided by 25 and multiplied by 10, giving 64 characters on one line.

Suitable margin settings in this case might be:
Left margin: 11
Right margin: 74 (64 characters from the left margin, including eleventh column)

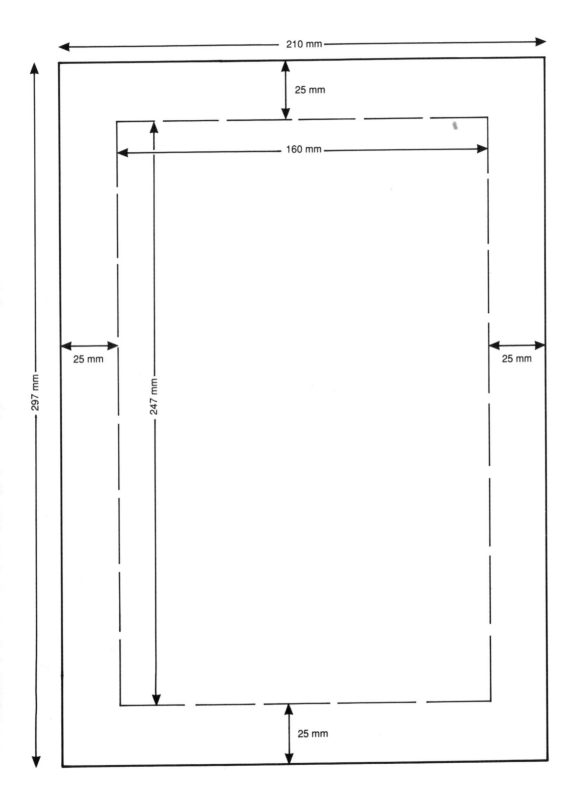

8. Applications

Almost any application requiring the manipulation of text can be handled efficiently with a word-processor. Only a few of the most common applications are described here.

Standard letters

These are letters containing the same information that are sent to many customers. With the merge printing facility the letters can be 'personalised', i.e. the name and address of the customer can be added to the letter. Matching envelope labels can also be printed.

Contracts and agreements

Most legal contracts contain standard information. When a solicitor's secretary prepares a contract, some of these paragraphs can be read into the document by using the stored paragraphs facility. The paragraphs need only be typed in once and can then be used any number of times.

Reports

Reports usually require a variety of presentation. Some of the various text enhancement facilities can be used here, as well as the ability of most word-processors to read text into the report from other sources, for example from a spreadsheet or data-base.

Mail shots

These are regular advertising leaflets posted to a compiled list of customers. The information may need to be changed from time to time, and word-processor editing facilities will help here. More importantly, the word-processor will produce printed labels showing the name and address of each customer.

Regularly updated lists

Lists of all kinds that require regular updating can be produced, such as price lists, directories, customer lists, inventories, and catalogues.

9. Advantages of word-processor use

We have already examined many of the advantages of word-processors in the creation and editing of documents of all kinds. Some of the most important advantages are summarised here.

Storage of text

The ability to store and retrieve text means that it can be used again, either exactly as first used or with changes. Magnetic storage media are also less bulky and easier to retrieve than paper copies.

Time savings

The ability to edit easily, both while entering text and subsequently, means a very significant saving in time, which is of great importance to a business.

Quality

The layout and general appearance of documents can be enhanced by changing typefaces, margins, alignment, and line spacing, as well as by other enhancement features, particularly if a high-quality printer such as a laser printer is available.

Security

Confidential documents are easily protected on word-processor files, which can be secured against accidental viewing or changing by use of the 'protect' tab on diskettes or programmed to require a password to permit viewing or changing them. Magnetic media can be easily stored in fireproof safes.

Ease of use

Most word-processor programs are easy to operate and learn. Good programs have a key that provides on-screen help when you are entering text.

10. Disadvantages of word-processor use

Despite their many advantages, word-processors have a number of drawbacks that should also be taken into account.

Cost

Business-quality computers and peripherals can be expensive, and the rapid pace of technological change can make systems obsolete very quickly.

Staff training

Staff must be trained to use the computers and the word-processor program. Equipment and programs will need to be upgraded occasionally and the staff retrained in their use. This can be a considerable cost for a business.

Poor checking

Because so many editing facilities are available during the typing of text, there may be a temptation to be less thorough in correcting the final print-out.

Health

There is some evidence that prolonged use of CRT monitors can have adverse physical effects (for example eye strain, migraine).

Summary

In this section we have examined the main features of a word-processor, and we hope that you have worked through all fifteen assignments on your own equipment and using your own programs. The word-processor is by far the most widely used computer application, and the ability to operate one is essential in many occupations as the trend away from the use of typewriters continues.

Questions

Multi-choice questions

1. Word-processing is:

   (a) the sending of text from a microcomputer to a large mainframe computer for processing
   (b) the use of microelectronic equipment to increase the amount of work carried out by office staff in a given time
   (c) the use of microelectronic equipment to enter, edit and store text
   (d) the use of microelectronic equipment to eliminate errors in writing?

2. Which of the following could be carried out just as efficiently using a typewriter as using a word-processor?

   (a) producing customised letters
   (b) producing short occasional letters
   (c) producing long legal documents with many identical clauses
   (d) producing complex medical documents containing many pharmaceutical terms

3. Centred text in a document may help to highlight:

   (a) text that has to be moved
   (b) the start of a new section
   (c) text that contains errors
   (d) where we must justify the text?

4. A triple-underline symbol on a corrected document means that we must:

   (a) start a new paragraph
   (b) use a capital letter
   (c) use a lower-case letter
   (d) correct the spelling of a word?

5. The 'find and replace' facility—

   (a) finds all occurrences of words longer than eight characters and offers a list of alternatives from the thesaurus
   (b) finds a block of text you may have marked for moving and allows you to replace the markers with 'move' symbols
   (c) searches for all words at the beginning of sentences and checks that they start with a capital letter
   (d) finds one or all occurrences of the given text and changes it to the given replacement?

6. The term 'pitch' in word-processing means:

   (a) the number of characters per 25 mm (1 in.)
   (b) the number of characters per line
   (c) the number of lines per page
   (d) the space between lines of type?

7. The term 'text' means:

(a) letters, numbers and symbols (excluding pictures and diagrams) that make up a document
(b) documents that consist of letters only
(c) all documents (excluding business letters)
(d) a document that does not contain any typing errors?

8. Which of the following would not be contained in the ruler line?

(a) the left margin setting
(b) the right margin setting
(c) the current position of the cursor
(d) the tab settings?

9. Many word-processors nowadays provide a 'WYSIWYG' display. This means:

(a) that the spelling check is automatically run on a document just before it is saved
(b) that the style and layout of a printed document will be the same as the display
(c) that the spelling check and thesaurus are executed together just before a document is saved
(d) that a number of documents can be queued and printed in sequence using the same command?

10. A notice is to be printed on A4 paper using 12-pitch type, with 25 mm (1 in.) margins all round and vertical spacing of 2.25 lines per centimetre (6 lines per inch). Which of the following sets of figures is correct?

	Left margin	Right margin	Number of text lines
(a)	12	99	58
(b)	12	87	52
(c)	13	99	66
(d)	13	87	58

Short-answer questions

1. Briefly describe the main text editing facilities of a word-processor.

2. Suggest three advantages and two disadvantages of a word-processor compared with a typewriter.

3. What is a special-purpose or 'dedicated' word-processor, and how does it differ from a microcomputer running a word-processor program?

4. Briefly describe the main features you would look for in buying a word-processor program.

5. Describe the following styles of text alignment, and give examples of where each one might be used: justified, flush left, flush right, and centred.

6. Distinguish between pitch and line spacing in relation to documents produced on a word-processor.

7. Describe, with the aid of diagrams, the different sizes of stationery used in word-processing.

8. Illustrate, by means of an example, the 'stored paragraphs' facility of a word-processor.

9. What is merge printing? Give an example of an application where it might be used.

10. Distinguish between the spelling check and thesaurus facilities of a word-processor.

Glossary of word-processing terms

alignment: the way in which the text of a document is adjusted relative to the left and right margins, whether flush left, flush right, justified, or centred.

bold type: a typeface design matching the one in normal use but made up of thicker lines to give emphasis; on dot-matrix printers, bold type is simulated by overstriking the same characters two or more times.

carriage return: the keystroke or command that ends the current line of text and sends the cursor to the first character position on the next line, invoked in word-processing by pressing the 'enter' key.

centred: the style of alignment in which the text is placed half way between the left and right margins of the document.

data file: a computer file on disk that contains text or other data that the user has created and stored, as distinct from program files, which contain the computer code that runs the program.

editing: making corrections and other changes to a text, including substitutions, deletions, and insertions.

'find and replace': a facility that automatically replaces a selected word or phrase with an alternative word or phrase, at selected occurrences or at every occurrence in the document.

flush left: the style of alignment in which lines are of different length and the text has a straight left margin and uneven right margin, exactly as it was typed into the word-processor.

flush right: the style of alignment in which lines are of different length and the text has a straight right margin and uneven left margin.

font: a special type of program file that contains instructions for creating a particular typeface on the printer, usually with a separate font for each size.

justification: the style of alignment in which all the lines are forced out to equal length by increasing the space between words, with straight left and right margins.

line spacing: the adjustable vertical distance between lines of text.

menu: a list of the options available at any stage in the execution of a program.

merge printing: a facility that allows the user to customise standard documents by automatically reading in variable data.

page break: a code in a word-processor file that causes the printer to start printing on a new page; it may be a 'forced page break' entered by the user or one that occurs automatically when the amount of text entered would fill the defined page size.

pitch: the number of characters printed horizontally per 25 mm (1 in.).

ruler line: a highlighted line at the top of a work area that defines the present position of the left and right margins and of any tabs that have been set.

special-purpose ('dedicated') word-processor: a computer specifically designed to perform word-processing tasks only, usually with the word-processor program contained in the ROM.

spelling check: a facility of most word-processors that checks the spelling of words in a document by comparing them against a list of words in one of the program files.

status line: a highlighted line at the top or bottom of a work area that shows the current position of the cursor and usually gives information about the file and certain program settings.

stored paragraph: a paragraph stored in a separate file on disk that can be combined with other paragraphs to make up a composite document.

tab key: a key that causes the cursor to jump a number of spaces horizontally to user-defined positions on the typing line in order to set the width of columns and the space between them.

thesaurus: a facility that allows the user to choose alternative words from lists of words with a related meaning.

typeface: a distinctive style of type with its own name.

underlining: the printing of a continuous line under a selected group of words to emphasise them.

word-processor: a computer program used in the creating, editing and printing of text.

word wraparound: a feature of a word-processor that causes the cursor to move automatically to the beginning of the next line in the display when the end of a line is reached.

work area: the area of the display excluding the status line, menu, and ruler line, where text is typed and edited.

Section E

Conclusion

Integrated packages

Microcomputer programs can be divided into three types according to the way in which they can be used in conjunction with other programs.

A 'standalone' program can be used for one application only—for example word-processing—and cannot incorporate files from other programs.

A 'non-standalone' program can also be used for only one application but has an 'import facility', which allows the user to include files from certain other applications: for example to import a spreadsheet from a spreadsheet program into a word-processor program in compiling a report.

An 'integrated package', on the other hand, contains a number of different applications, all within the same main program. Typical combinations include a word-processor, a data-base, and a spreadsheet, and sometimes a communications program and a graphics program. These packages allow the user to import or export data files between applications; and—unlike the non-standalone programs—if data is changed in one application, the data change will be reflected in all related applications, so that, for example, a graph made up with spreadsheet data would change automatically to reflect recalculations on the spreadsheet.

Advantages of integrated packages

Integrated packages have a number of advantages over other types of program.

One program for most essential applications

An integrated package allows the user to produce all the usual business documents using only one program.

Easy to learn and use

Instead of having to become familiar with the conventions and commands of four or five different programs, the user has the advantage of a common method of entering commands; for example, the command to save data to a disk would be the same for all the applications in the program. Once the commands and conventions of the program are mastered the user will only have to learn the underlying concept of the different applications to use the program.

Cost

There can be a large cost saving with an integrated package compared with the cost of purchasing four or five standalone application programs.

Disadvantages of integrated package use

Integrated packages also have a number of significant disadvantages, however.

Less advanced features

Applications in an integrated package contain less advanced features than standalone programs. Integrated packages never have enough memory to contain all the advanced features of standalone programs.

Limited space for data files

The packages occupy a large amount of RAM, limiting the size of data files that can be used.

ASSIGNMENT

In this book, one particular application was used to carry out each assignment: a data-base, spreadsheet or word-processor program. There are, however, many situations where the computer user may use a combination of all three to carry out a particular task.

The following assignment is an example, where all three applications are used to generate a useful report. You may use standalone programs, non-standalone programs or an integrated package to complete the assignment.

Comfort Footwear PLC was established in Cork in 1974 by Peter Casey. The company manufactures a mid-range sports training shoe: the Marathon Marvel. Market research shows that it is bought mainly by people under the age of 25. The sales price is £25.50.

The company has its head office in Cork, but it supplies its products to retail shops throughout the country. The following market information is available to the marketing director of the company:

1. Competitors' sales

There are five competitor companies importing a similar type of sports shoe. The table below outlines the number of pairs of mid-range sports training shoes sold by Comfort Footwear and each of the competitor companies during the past year.

Table 1				
Company	Connacht	Leinster	Munster	Ulster
Comfort Footwear	4,400	32,200	21,200	3,500
Allweather Shoes	4,000	38,000	8,200	8,400
John Martin	8,700	46,000	17,800	18,600
Easyfeet Now	1,700	9,400	12,100	6,900
J. K. Williams and Son	5,500	24,000	4,800	44,500
Footwear Supplies	700	5,600	4,200	2,450

2. Market population structure

The following table shows a percentage breakdown of the population of Ireland by province and age group for 1990:

Table 2				
Age group	Connacht	Leinster	Munster	Ulster
Under 15	2	12	4	3
16 to 25	2	20	3	7
26 to 60	4	13	7	10
Over 60	1	6	3	3

3. Company sales trends

The next table shows the total number of units sold by each of the six companies in four consecutive years:

Table 3				
Company	1988	1989	1990	1991
Comfort Footwear	33,000	34,550	47,800	61,300
Allweather Shoes	45,000	38,700	47,400	58,600
John Martin	30,000	80,500	62,000	49,700
Easyfeet Now	20,000	29,600	31,800	30,100
J. K. Williams and Son	45,000	92,500	83,600	78,800
Footwear Supplies		13,400	12,300	12,950

4. The sales team

The company's sales team consists of the following twelve members:

Seán McCarthy has been with the company since its foundation. He is based in Cork. His sales for the past year were 8,300 units. The total distance covered by Seán to achieve these sales was 93,000 km, and he incurred £6,200 in expenses.

Ronan Byrne joined the company at the beginning of the year after completing his Sales and Management Diploma at the College of Commerce in Rathmines, Dublin. Ronan is based in the Carlow-Kilkenny region. The total distance covered in the course of his work was 45,000 km, and his expenses amounted to £3,400. For the past year Ronan's total sales amounted to 3,600 units.

Catherine Stephens joined the company in 1988 after gaining three years' experience in sales with John Martin Ltd. She is attached to the company's Dublin office, and her sales for the past year amounted to 7,500 units. Catherine's total travelling amounted to 35,000 km, and she had £2,400 of expenses.

Linda O'Connor has been with the company since 1985, and is responsible for sales in north Leinster. She was ill for three months during the year but still managed to sell 4,800 units. She had £3,900 of expenses and she travelled 29,000 km in the course of her work.

Brian Ward, a native of Castlebar, is our sole sales representative in Connacht. He joined the company in 1982 after three years as a member of the Garda Síochána. His sales for the past year were 4,400 units. During the year Brian travelled 75,000 km to achieve his sales, and had expenses of £5,100.

Claire Conroy joined the company in 1986 after returning from the United States, where she gained two years' valuable experience in selling and sales management with a large pharmaceutical company in San Francisco. She is attached to the company's Dublin office, and her sales for the past year were 6,800 units. She covered 50,000 km in making her sales, and her expenses were £5,800.

Liam Dolan, a native of Co. Kerry but now living in Waterford, has been with the company since 1988. His sales for the past year in Munster were 5,700 units. Liam travelled 145,000 km to make his sales, and he had expenses of £5,900.

Kevin Molloy is our sole sales representative in Ulster. He joined the company in 1981 after resigning his teaching position at a secondary school in Omagh. He was a successful member of the Leinster sales team, and this year he has been redeployed to the Ulster region. This is the first year that the company is selling the product in Ulster. Kevin's sales in Ulster amounted to 3,500 units for the past year. Kevin had expenses of £2,700, and he covered 38,000 km in the course of his work.

Peter McNicholl is another member of our Leinster sales team. He has been with the company since 1979, and his sales for the past year were 5,300 units. Peter had £4,100 expenses during the year and covered 50,000 km to achieve his sales.

Rachel Doyle, a native of Dublin but now living in Co. Tipperary, is responsible for sales in north Munster. She joined the company in 1985 on her return from Glasgow, where she worked for one year as a member of the sales team of a cosmetics company. She was attached to Comfort Footwear's Dublin office until 1989. Her sales amounted to 4,000 units for the past year. Rachel's travelling for the company during the year was 42,000 km, and her expenses amounted to £3,300.

Jim Ellis joined the company in 1987 after spending three years with Allweather Shoes as a member of their sales team. His sales in Munster for the past year were 3,200 units. Jim had to travel 37,000 km for the company during the year, and his expenses were £3,600.

Brenda Scott joined the company in 1984 as secretary to the managing director, and in 1987 she joined the sales team, of which she is now an effective member. She operates in Kildare, Wicklow, and Wexford, and her sales for the past year were 4,200 units. Brenda's travelling for the company during the year totalled 35,000 km, and she had expenses of £2,400.

Carry out the following tasks:

You are required to generate a report for the managing director of Comfort Footwear, using the following applications programs: data-base, spreadsheet, graphics (if available), and word-processor.

Outputs from the data-base, spreadsheet and graphics programs are to be included in the appendixes of the report (if you are using standalone programs). Comments and explanations marked with an asterisk (*) are to be produced using the word-processor program, making reference to the appendixes. (If you are using an integrated package, the word 'output' will refer to output files that will be integrated into the report. If you are using standalone programs, 'outputs' will refer to print-outs obtained.)

The report must be divided into two sections:

Section A: General sales report

In compiling the general sales report you must take the following steps:

[1] Enter the data from table 3 into a spreadsheet; you should then use this spreadsheet to show:

(a) the overall sales in Ireland of mid-range sports training shoes for each year, and

(b) the percentage market share for each company for each year, using the overall sales calculated above.

[2] Produce *two* line graphs, one showing the number of units sold for each company and the other showing the percentage market share for each company for the four-year period. These graphs can be obtained by using the graphics capability of your speadsheet program, or otherwise.

[3] Include this spreadsheet and these graphs as appendix A in the report.

*[4] Comment on the percentage market share for each company and the changing trend in units sold.

[5] Enter the data from table 1 into a spreadsheet, showing total units sold in each province, and show the percentage market share in each province for each company during the past year.

[6] Include this spreadsheet as appendix B in the report.

*[7] With reference to appendix B:

(a) indicate the company with the highest market share in each province, and

(b) show how the companies have spread their sales across the provinces, and which seems the most successful policy.

Section B: Sales team report

In compiling the sales team report you must take the following steps:

[1] Enter the information on Comfort Footwear's sales team into a data-base file. Each record in the file should contain the following fields for each salesperson as given in the sales personnel data above:

> (a) name (surname first);
>
> (b) province;
>
> (c) sales (units) during 1991;
>
> (d) expenses incurred during 1991;
>
> (e) distance travelled for 1991;
>
> (f) number of years' sales experience (including experience with other companies) to the end of 1991.

[2] Extract from this data-base file an output list of the sales personnel, sorted in descending order of the number of units sold by each salesperson in 1991, together with their respective province and number of years' experience.

[3] Include this output list as appendix C in the report.

*[4] Comment on the relationship between unit sales achieved and the number of years' sales experience of the members of the sales team.

[5] Extract from the data-base file an output list showing name, sales and province of all sales staff who did not reach the company's sales quota of 5,000 units during 1991, sorted in alphabetical order of name. Include this list as appendix D in the report.

*[6] In each case where the sales quota was not reached, comment on possible reasons, other than sales experience, with particular reference to population structure (table 2) and competition in each region (table 1, and appendixes A and B).

[7] extract from the data-base file an output list showing the name, distance travelled, sales and province of the entire sales team, sorted in descending order of distance travelled. Include this list as appendix E in the report.

*[8] After you have examined appendix E, consider whether there is a stronger relationship between distance travelled and sales in certain provinces.

[9] Extract from the data-base file an output list showing the name and distance travelled, in descending order of distance covered during 1991, of those sales personnel who are exempt from 'benefit in kind' tax (see question 12 below). Include this list as appendix F in the report.* Explain that the sales personnel in appendix F are exempt from benefit-in-kind tax, and explain why.

[10] Produce an output list in alphabetical order of surname for each member of the sales team showing name, sales experience, distance travelled, and unit sales. (appendix G)

[11] Using the output list from appendix G above, enter on a spreadsheet the name, sales experience, distance travelled and unit sales for each member of the sales team for 1991.

[12] Sales representatives using company cars can be liable for 'benefit in kind' tax. The aim of this tax is to discourage people from registering cars for business purposes and then using them largely for private purposes.

The tax is calculated as a percentage of the value of the car. Those who travel more than 40,234 km (25,000 miles) in one year are exempt from this tax. For those whose annual travelling was less than 40,234 km the tax is calculated as follows:

For each successive 1,609 km (1,000 miles) less than 40,234 an extra 2 per cent of the car's value is charged as tax; for example, a salesperson who has a car valued at £10,000 and a total travelling distance in one year of 37,000 km would pay £400 tax:

Rate of tax = ((40,234 – 37,000) ÷ 1,609) X 0.02 = 0.04
Amount of tax = 0.04 X 10,000 = £400

The following general formulas can be used:

$$\text{Tax rate} = ((40234 - distance)/1609)*0.02$$
$$\text{Tax amount} = tax\ rate * value\ of\ car$$

Set up a new column showing the 'benefit in kind' tax for each member of Comfort Footwear's sales team. (Assume each salesperson drives a car valued £12,500.)

[13] Set up a SALES VALUE column in the spreadsheet, showing the total sales value for each salesperson by multiplying the number of units sold by the unit retail price.

[14] Set up a VARIANCE column, to contain the difference in unit sales and the company's 1991 sales quota (5,000 units) for each of the sales personnel.

[15] As an incentive to its sales team the company operates the following bonus scheme: those who sell more than the sales quota will receive 5 per cent of the unit price as a bonus for each unit sold over the quota. Set up a BONUS column to display the total bonus, if any, paid to each member of the sales team.

[16] Each member of the sales team receives a basic salary of £10,000 and a further £500 for each year's sales experience. Set up a SALARY column to include these salary details.

[17] Commission is calculated on the basis of 1 per cent of sales value. Set up a COMMISSION column to show the commission paid to each of the sales personnel.

[18] The total income of each salesperson is calculated by adding the salary, commission, and any bonus earned. Include an INCOME column to show the total income of each member of the sales team in the past year.

[19] Include this spreadsheet as appendix H in the report.

*[20] Outline in the report the method of calculating the bonus, salary, and commission, and give a full explanation of 'benefit in kind' tax.